Worth Fighting For

Worth Fighting For

An Army Ranger's Journey Out of the Military and Across America

Rory Fanning

Haymarket Books
Chicago, Illinois

Published in 2014 by
Haymarket Books
P.O. Box 180165
Chicago, IL 60618
773-583-7884
info@haymarketbooks.org
www.haymarketbooks.org

ISBN: 978-1-60846-391-6

Trade distribution:
In the US, Consortium Book Sales and Distribution, www.cbsd.com
In the UK, Turnaround Publisher Services, www.turnaround-uk.com
In Canada, Publishers Group Canada, www.pgcbooks.ca
All other countries, Publishers Group Worldwide, www.pgw.com

Special discounts are available for bulk purchases by organizations and institutions. Please contact Haymarket Books for more information at 773-583-7884 or info@haymarketbooks.org.

Cover design by Eric Ruder.

This book was published with the generous support of the Wallace Action Fund and Lannan Foundation.

Printed in Canada by union labor.

Library of Congress CIP data is available.

10 9 8 7 6 5 4 3 2 1

To fight that war they would need men, and if men saw the future they wouldn't fight. So they were masking the future, they were keeping the future a soft, quiet, deadly secret. They knew that if all the little people, all the little guys saw the future they would begin to ask questions. They would ask questions and they would find answers, and they would say to the guys who wanted them to fight, they would say, you lying thieving sons-of-bitches we won't fight we won't be dead, we will live, we are the world, we are the future, and we will not let you butcher us no matter what you say, no matter what speeches you make, no matter what slogans you write. Remember it well, we are the world we are what makes it go round, we make bread and cloth; and guys, we are the hub of the wheel and the spokes of the wheel itself, without us you would be hungry naked worms and we will not die.

—Dalton Trumbo, *Johnny Got His Gun*

Contents

Introduction

FORT BENNING, GA

March 23, 2003, 6:30 a.m.

On a sunny but brisk March morning in Georgia, I was feeling divided over whether or not I was doing the right thing for myself, my country, and the world by fighting the global "War on Terror" as an Army Ranger. It was after a workout and I was standing in line waiting for permission to enter a military cafeteria, along with a few dozen other soldiers. We stared at the ground, hungry and mostly silent as our warm breath hung in the air. I had returned to the US only a few weeks before, after a nine-month tour in Afghanistan.

A tan Humvee drove up and stopped at the end of the sidewalk where we stood. The window rolled down and we all heard, "Hey Tillman, drop and give me twenty." The sergeant who had barked the order smiled a sinister smile. Tillman, who was standing a few feet from me, fell to the ground without hesitation and snapped out twenty strong, sharp push-ups, then stood up and, for a moment, stared at the sergeant who gave the order.

Pat Tillman broke no rules that morning. The sergeant wanted to show him who was in charge. When being disciplined by a higher-ranking non-commissioned officer, most privates and specialists look back at the officer with dead eyes, showing complete submission. Not Pat. Pat looked back with a moral authority and confidence that transcended rank. Pat towered over the sergeant in that instant. The sergeant's command now looked hollow and forced—the opposite of intimidating. He drove off.

Standing in the chow-hall line, Pat reminded me that the military is composed of people, not robots. We followed orders, we did what we were told, but it was only because we gave the higher ranks permission. Pat's look showed me that we could stop the orders at any time. Pat Tillman was the first person to suggest to me that it was possible to stand up to the US military.

Pat and I never had the opportunity to become close. He and his brother Kevin were kind to me while I was going through a traumatic experience in the military and feeling utterly alone. I idealized them both because of that. But the fact remains that I am alive today, or at least less damaged, because of Pat Tillman.

Pat was killed by friendly fire in southwest Afghanistan in late April 2004. The military, scared of the fallout from the story, lied to those of us in the Ranger Battalion who weren't at the scene—and then to the rest of the world—about the circumstances of his death. They told us Pat died as the result of an enemy ambush. They lied. The cover-up was extensive and painted Pat as a poster boy for the War on Terror. A notebook in which he had sketched out some of his thoughts about the war was burned, along with his body armor. When the lies became public, there was a media firestorm; in response, Pat's mother Mary Tillman wrote a terrific book called *Boots on the Ground by Dusk*. Anyone interested in Pat's complete story should pick it up.

I was a conscientious objector the day Pat Tillman was killed. I had been in a six-month limbo, waiting to be sent to jail or to the "big army" to become a "bullet stopper." Pat Tillman is the only reason I was allowed to leave the military. I was released seven days after his death, on my birthday. I didn't know why at the time, but the chain of command in my battalion had no time for me anymore.

I walked across the country for a lot of reasons. For one thing, I was trying to get my mind right. I wanted to be alone to think things through. I needed the option to interact with people if I chose to. Passing through towns on foot, with an excuse to stay or leave people, would give me a chance to gauge any developments and growth the walking would afford me. I also knew the value of good old-fashioned masochism. If I couldn't learn to understand my mental tics, I'd diffuse them by walking with a lot of weight strapped to my back. The military had left me overwhelmed in the presence of strangers and even my friends and family. I knew I had to do something about that if I was ever going to feel a degree of self-possession in the company of others. Seeing a therapist never felt like an option: the thought of letting a stranger see the size and shape of my brain always felt like a violation of some unspoken self-sufficiency code. I was lost and didn't know how to ask for directions.

I also walked across the country because I wanted to see and learn as much as I could about the country I felt I had let down by quitting the military. Guilt, betrayal, a sense of adventure, ignorance, a desire to be accepted, pride, and promoting the legacy of a person who needed to be remembered: these were all reasons I decided I should hit the road.

As in the military, there had to be rules. I had to carry everything on my back, like I knew my friends deployed in Afghanistan and Iraq were doing. I had to stay as disciplined as I could—I had to walk every step from the Atlantic to the Pacific. No rides forward. If I did receive a ride to a house, a restaurant, or a must-see location, I would be dropped off in the exact spot where I had been picked up. I carried a single-person tent, a sleeping bag, a sleeping mat, and a BlackBerry, on which I took notes and posted to my blog at walkforpat.org.

I carried a sign:

> Rory Fanning, who served in the Second Army Ranger Battalion with Pat Tillman, is walking from the Atlantic to the Pacific to raise money for the Pat Tillman Foundation. Visit walkforpat.org for information on how you can help.

I also carried a GPS device so people could follow my progress, two pairs of pants, ten pairs of socks, personal hygiene equipment, fifty yards of parachute rope, a winter hat, an iPod, gloves, baby wipes, a picture of my girlfriend Kate, an outdated laptop—which I would send home six days into the walk—and a hat with the number 42 on it. (Forty-two was Pat's football jersey number at Arizona State.) I would later be given countless trinkets and mementoes, including the keys to a few cities and some Star Wars figures. The pack weighed between forty-five and fifty-five pounds for most of the walk.

Pat Tillman made a sacrifice for a cause bigger than his immediate material interest. He gave up millions for a shitty job. I thought his example could be an example to others in a country divided by enormous inequality in wealth and power. My goal was to raise $3.6 million: the value of the contract Pat gave up when he joined the military. I found that people from every walk of life donated what they could, whether that was thousands of dollars, a handful of change, or an entire shift's tips.

When I returned from the walk I had a strong need to go back and retrace my steps via history books. I wanted to know as much about the history of these states as possible. I felt connected to the land in the US but I also knew that the mini-malls, the asphalt, and even the trees I walked by, over, and through didn't tell the whole story—far from it. The people I met were products of history, and there was much to learn from them. I did garner some historical information, but I didn't feel like I was getting the whole story. So I did my best to uncover as much as I could about the roads I took and the states I walked through when I got home. I have shared some of it with you in this book, through brief sections in each chapter. These are stories about other kinds of conscientious objectors, of people who gave their all for a cause, people who thought long and hard about what was right—people like Pat.

Over the past decade, since leaving the military and finishing the walk, I have gone from a devout Christian to an atheist and from a conservative Republican to a socialist. My time in the military and the cover-up of Pat's death led me down a road that challenged the core of who I was. I began to question everything—and ended up here. I feel like I have uncovered a lot since then; I hope this book inspires you to uncover the hidden things in your life as well.

Part I

CHICAGO O'HARE INTERNATIONAL AIRPORT

September 17, 2008

"What can I throw out?"

My new blue Deuter backpack was placed on a large stainless steel scale at the check-in counter at O'Hare Airport. The scale flashed: forty-nine pounds. I knew it would be close—if your bag weighs more than fifty pounds, they hit you for another fifty dollars. In addition to nearly every song Woody Guthrie ever recorded, it held my house, bed, clothes, and a few other necessities for the next nine months. I was leaving Chicago with as little as possible to walk across the country for Pat Tillman, a man with whom I'd had perhaps a dozen conversations. The whole thing felt strange, new, and exhilarating.

On the plane, time slipped away like a handful of ocean water. I'd quit my job at the bank the week before, less than a month before the stock-market crash that kicked off what came to be known as the Great Recession. The wheels bounced to the ground. My pack and I were in a hazy and humid Norfolk, Virginia.

1

Virginia

VIRGINIA BEACH, VA | Mile 0

Population 437,994 | Est. 1906

> *For exile hath more terror in his look, much more than death: do not say "banishment."*
>
> —**William Shakespeare,** *Romeo and Juliet*

A cab pulled to the curb of the terminal. I hopped in and said, "Take me to the ocean."

"The ocean is a big place. Where specifically?" the driver replied.

"It doesn't matter. I'm on a budget, so take the fastest route."

He shrugged and started driving. I rolled down the window to let the late-summer wind erase my uneasy thoughts.

Mike Gooding, a reporter from Norfolk's ABC affiliate, met me a few feet from the water on Virginia Beach to ask me about my walk and the Pat Tillman Foundation. The foundation thought my plan was interesting and worth supporting, but I sensed an apprehension in their endorsement. They were and are rightly protective of Pat Tillman's name. I could understand why they didn't want people co-opting Pat's life for self-interested reasons, as so many others have done.

Gooding asked why I was walking across the country. I felt like a ventriloquist was forcing me to respond. "I want to raise $3.6 million for the Pat Tillman Foundation—the contract Pat Tillman, the former NFL star turned down to join the military. . . . This country needs more people to make decisions like Pat's . . ." I stumbled.

A more thorough answer would have gone something like this:

Four years before, I had been in purgatory with the US military—the Second Army Ranger Battalion. After two deployments to Afghanistan, I had become one of the first Rangers, if not *the* first Ranger, to formally reject my unit's orders to Iraq and Afghanistan. I was a conscientious objector. For six months, while they figured out what to do with me, I painted curbs yellow, scrubbed grills, baked cake, cut grass, washed dishes, and absorbed the ridicule of my chain of command. I did my best to numb myself and saw the world as if looking out of binoculars through the wrong end—everything felt small and distant.

Occasionally I'd see a demeaning smirk or hear "Pussy!" in the chow hall as I served my former comrades. Sometimes I became lost in their ideas of what it meant to be a man: I would drop my eyes and they'd feel stronger. At quieter moments, I lay in the dark on a sheetless mattress with an old sweatshirt as my pillow and wondered which of them could do what I was doing.

Rejecting the mission of a Ranger was like rejecting your brother. Rangers stick together. They do not question authority. Those who do are outcasts. In the Rangers' world, there are two types of men: Rangers and civilians. Rangers are courageous, honorable, strong, and determined. Civilians are cowardly, undisciplined, and weak. I now fell into the civilian category. This made it hard to trust my decision.

I hopped on a plane for Chicago and went AWOL after six months of punishment detail to force a hand on my case—and to see a woman I'd been talking to. I returned after five days and a heated phone conversation with the sergeant major. "Get your motherfucking ass back here—now!" he screamed. Forcing a confident tone, I said, from a busy street corner in Chicago, "You don't get to tell me what to do anymore. If I come back it's because I want to, not because of anything you say." No one spoke to the sergeant major that way.

When I returned to the battalion on the morning of April 21, I was immediately arrested. Getting arrested for wanting to quit your job felt like a joke—a joke that scared the shit out of me. I walked into my squad's common area, where on many nights we participated in after-action reports and talked about how best to engage the enemy. I was wearing jeans and a T-shirt. The walls were cinder-block. Green military bags and equipment were crammed into corners. The arresting sergeant was my squad leader. He stood before me along with a few other sergeants, all of them dressed in full fatigues. They read me my military rights: "You have a right to an attorney . . . anything you say can be used against you. . . . You are now confined to the room until further notice."

Then they left me alone for about six hours. A Groucho Marx quote ran through my head: "Military justice is to justice as military music is to music." I expected the worst.

The sun set and the room became dark. A young sergeant eventually came back. "What the hell are you sitting in the dark for?" He flipped on the fluorescent lights. He was told to tell me that I could go back to my room but couldn't leave the building. I would soon be sent to jail or the "big army" shortly.

The "big army" is a term used for any infantry military assignment outside of the Special Forces—of which the Rangers are part. If you were a member of the big army you were more expendable because you had less training and could be readily replaced. You were what the Rangers would call a "bullet stopper." To the high-ranking brass, soldiers are no different than Humvees, infrared goggles, or any other piece of expensive military equipment—but the more training you receive, the more money you're worth, and no one wants to be accountable for the loss of an expensive piece of equipment.

So the big army seemed like a death sentence—but in some ways death felt comparable to jail.

They said my true story would leave me forever banished from the good graces of future employers. They said I'd be banished in a country I had once adored. They said I'd be shunned by my family and friends.

The next morning, I was called to a formation. "Pat Tillman was killed last night in an enemy ambush in southwest Afghanistan," said the sergeant in charge of the "rear detachment"—those who were injured, on their way out of the military, or in trouble. "He died a hero, doing what he was trained to do." My stomach dropped and tears welled in my eyes. Pat was larger than life. It made no sense. A dark cloud settled over the battalion. I sat in my room, staring out the window, wanting to talk to others about the terrible and surreal news. I was ostracized, so I couldn't.

Six days later, on my birthday, my discharge papers were signed. It would have happened three days sooner, but I pushed back against the chain of command's attempt to issue a dishonorable discharge. There are three discharge statuses in the military: honorable, general, and dishonorable. I told the commanding officer, "I'll stay and fight a dishonorable discharge. I've already spoken to the Inspector General's office. They know protocol was not followed in the handling of my case." They gave in after only a little harassment. It was clear they just wanted to get rid of me. There would be no big army, no jail, no punishment, no big discussion—save the humiliation I would endure the rest of my life for abandoning my Ranger buddies, at least according to the parting comments of my company commander from West Point. They made me sign a paper saying that the Ranger Battalion had followed protocol in the handling of my case.

But I didn't say any of that to Mike Gooding. I didn't know yet why I had to walk—not really.

I left the ocean at 2:30 in the afternoon. It didn't feel like I had permission to be doing what I was doing—who from, I don't know. The bank? The military? My family? The expansive view from the plane was etched in my brain—I was on an Earth-sized hamster wheel. Highway 4, leading west away from the ocean, cut through a dense pine forest. It was with a detached energy that I took those first steps, the weight of my pack dragging on me. I was not in my body, or so it seemed.

The only thing I can remember thinking about while walking that day was my girlfriend Kate. We had been living together. I was sure she would leave me. Who would stick with someone who said he had to walk across the country before getting married? My walk would take only a little less time than my first tour to Afghanistan: nine months. I pretended it wouldn't take that long. The Google Maps walking directions said three months.

It took me a few years to tell Kate about my time in the military. Despite that, when the military came up, she had a graceful touch. She always knew when to change the topic or ask the next right question.

I asked her how she felt about the walk. She said, "I can wait three months."

She let me keep my things in the apartment. I told her I would call her every day.

First Landing State Park, Virginia

The first Africans landed in Virginia as indentured servants in 1619. Over the years, thousands of shackled men, women, and children were forced off impossibly cramped ships and onto these shores, destined for a life of violence and misery.

Nat Turner, the preacher, conspirator, and revolutionary, led a slave revolt in late August 1831 in the woods and open fields where I walked. Turner wrote in his autobiography, "When I walked through the fields I saw blood in the leaves and heard the wailing of voices in the winds."[1] He presided over funerals and prayer services, where he conspired with and recruited other slaves for rebellion. On August 13 there was a solar eclipse over Virginia—and Turner saw it as his signal to begin the revolt. The plan was for Turner and fifty other slaves to raid a large arms depot, attack the larger plantations, and escape to the Great Dismal Swamp—now a wildlife refuge—to recruit other slaves and lead more raids. Turner's band was soon met with resistance. Outnumbered, they retreated to a nearby cave and hid for six weeks. Virginia was crippled with fear as whites agonized over Turner's next move. Anyone found sympathizing with the revolt, white or Black, was savagely beaten or imprisoned for sedition. Turner was eventually caught on October 30 and hung on November 11, 1831.[2]

NORFOLK, VIRGINIA | Mile 19

Population 242,803 | Est. 1705

Restless, I woke up at four in the morning and packed quickly. Power-walking over bridges and cutting across parks, I made my way through Norfolk in the early morning darkness. Adrenaline and suppressed doubt filled me while the Atlantic breeze kept me cool. For the first time in my life, I wanted to run away from the ocean. "I'll know I'm serious after a day or two. I need a thirty- or forty-mile buffer between me and the ocean," I said to myself.

My interview with Mike Gooding got me noticed. Locals began to honk their horns and wave soon after the sun declared the day. Two sixteen-year-old girls with matching KISS T-shirts saw me and asked for autographs on a box of Royal Cups cigarettes and a recently graded high-school history exam. Soon after, two middle-aged Black women with ankle-length skirts and cups of McDonald's coffee gave me Bible literature and two dollars. Further down the road, a man named Tim Howard pulled over and prayed with his hand on my shoulder. A policewoman, Jennifer Dozier, and her partner asked what I was doing and, after talking awhile, drove off. They met me again further down the road; Officer Dozier jumped out and ran a prayer card over to me. Her brother Jonathan had been killed nine months earlier in Iraq, she said, and with tears in her eyes asked if I would carry his card to the Pacific. Thinking about Jonathan and my decision to leave the military, I looked up and found myself nineteen miles from the Atlantic.

A FEW MILES OUTSIDE OF CHESAPEAKE, VA | Mile 25

Highway 13 blends in very subtly with Route 58, which, according to state patrolman Craig, "is an interstate." He asked me, "Where are you going?"

"The A-A-Atlantic," I said.

"Well, you are going the wrong way," he said, in his best police voice.

"I mean, I'm walking to the Pacific for the Pat Tillman Foundation."

He warmed up, but didn't let me hold my course. He gave me a fifteen-minute explanation of an alternate route which involved retracing two miles of steps, crossing a junkyard, and using "your military skills."

"I appreciate your help, officer. I'm sorry for walking on the interstate," I said.

We parted and I backtracked half a mile east, wondering how I would ever walk across the country with such impersonal interruptions. When he was gone, I turned around and crossed to the opposite side of the same interstate. I jogged into the grass by the shoulder and walked west, down a steep embankment into the forest.

The woods were filled with razor-sharp vines and bogs. In less than thirty minutes I'd had enough of the mud and scratching and moved back to the grass. Patrolman Craig was issuing a ticket a hundred yards down the road. His one-way mirrored aviators signaled to me in the sun. I ran back into the woods and hid in a five-foot drainage tunnel, entertaining myself by checking to see if Kate had called. She hadn't.

Assuming Craig was finished and looking above instead of below me, I stepped out of the tunnel—and fell into a four-foot moat of sewer water. My pants, shoes, and half my pack were soaked in sludge that smelled like rotting teeth. I had duct-taped both sides of a plastic Ziploc sandwich bag to keep my wallet and cell phone dry—an old military trick. I splashed and fought against the suction of the bog and, after twenty minutes, slithered out of the warm slime to see that patrolman Craig was gone. I squished for three miles in the center median, well protected by a few long rows of trees as my mind edged toward a cliff. I could see down to the deepest reaches of my stupidity and it was frightening. Why had I ever thought walking across the country was a good idea?

FRANKLIN, VA | Mile 60

Population 8,582 | Est. 1876

My legs and shoulders cursed me as I set up my tent for the night. As I secured the last extension on the pole of my tent, the middle link shattered beyond repair. I settled into the semi-collapsed tent and called Uncle Dan's Outdoor Shop in Chicago, where I'd bought my gear. They had given me a significant discount and I felt guilty asking for more, but they agreed to overnight a new pole to me. Delayed already—a sign of things to come?

The tent pole arrived at 11:30 the next morning, and I was on the road by 1:00. Route 671 is the kind of lonely country road I envisioned spending most of my time on when I'd imagined the trip. The cotton farms reminded me of the brightly colored poppy fields in Afghanistan, which had startled me with their sinister, otherworldly beauty. Cotton in the raw is soft, white, and beady. I was listening to Ray Charles when I picked my first cotton "boll." He sang about steaks he could never afford and the girl he would never kiss. I thought how something so soft could put so much wealth in hands that did none of the picking and planting. I thought about the wars that had been fought over cotton, the backbreaking work it demanded. I thought of the bloody birth of the nation I now walked through.

I stopped by a peanut farm and shop ten miles outside of Franklin, where Blair and his father Charlie, a convivial older man with skin that resembled the peanut shells all around us, invited me to stay in their cabin and have a home-cooked meal. I happily agreed. They knew about Pat Tillman. Blair offered me a ride to his property two miles away but, mindful to walk every step to the Pacific, I said I would walk if that was okay. He left to tell his wife I was coming and I said goodbye to Charlie. A mile later, Blair pulled up next to me. I quickly apologized for not walking fast enough.

He said, "No problem. You can't come over. My wife won't let you. I tried to reason with her, sayin', 'I'll shoot his ass if he pulls anything, honey,' but she would have none of it."

"I completely understand. My girlfriend Kate back home would have said the same thing," I lied. He gave me ten bags of fresh peanuts for the road.

2

North Carolina

SEABOARD, NC | Mile 93

Population 612 | Est. 1877

I crossed the border into North Carolina. I had been walking for thirteen days. The Thursday-morning breakfast crowd was quiet as I fumbled into Broadland's Diner, wet and burdened by my oversized backpack and shepherd's staff. It had rained the previous night and into that morning. I heard whispers: "Where he come from?" "Who's that?" The walls were lime green and the linoleum floor was gray and cracking. The cook, who reminded me of Paul Robeson, broke the silence by asking an elderly lady in a powder-blue jumpsuit if she wanted butter on her oatmeal. She replied, "Child, now don't go makin' me lose my religion." Hungrily or gluttonously—growing up a guilty Catholic I always confused the two—I ordered French toast, a Western omelet, bacon, sausage, an egg, toast, potatoes, and coffee. When the cook, whose name I would later learn was Johnny Lassiter, served my three Styrofoam plates of breakfast, he asked where I was going. I told him where and why and we talked about the weather. I ate the food and drank the coffee in one big gulp, then stared at the wall, not wanting to get up. Johnny took the single step from the grill to the register and said, "I've been running short on my charitable contributions lately. You don't have to pay for your meal."

On the road after breakfast, a lump still in my throat from Johnny's kindness, a pit bull ran toward me. He crossed the street, slowed about ten feet behind me, and, like a jaguar, crouched and slunk closer. I grabbed my staff, ready to defend all that I owned, and continued to walk away, expecting the worst. A group of teenagers approached in an old Buick, gawking at the sight of most likely one of the few tourists ever to visit their neighborhood. As they gawked, their car slammed into the pit bull they weren't watching—all I heard was the thud. The car sped away. The dog squealed. Hit from the rear, he dragged himself back home by his front legs. The sound of the impact made me wonder if he was running home to die. I debated following the dog to make sure he was okay, but continued on my way.

The staff would be a faithful companion. I had received it an hour before sunset on the first day of the walk. I'd walked seven miles to a sand-carpeted and pine-filled First Landing State Park. Seagulls squawked overhead. I was feet from the Chesapeake Bay, which was pockmarked with barges. I met a white-haired man named John who ran the camp store. The store had a handmade birdcage, with a sign above the door that read "Home is Where You Start From." I explained what I was doing in the same nervous voice I'd used with the reporters. A smile came to his face and he said, in a slow, calm voice, "We need to take care of you." He went in the back of the store and came out with a six-foot-tall wooden shepherd's staff. I had chocolate, cans of soup, and Gatorade on the counter. He pointed to it all and said, "That is on the house. But you should really try the dry food in the back corner. It will carry lighter." I didn't want the dry food because it was too expensive and reminded me of the military. He insisted that I take some and that it was on the house as well. He lifted the staff over the cash register and put it in my hand. I was embarrassed when he wouldn't accept money. And thrilled—with everything but the walking stick. It seemed more of a souvenir than something I could use. It was made of heavy pine, as tall as I was. I was hoping to avoid attention, at least initially, until I settled into the idea of the walk. The blue turtle shell of a pack I would carry for almost nine months was awkward enough. John said I needed to take the staff: it would help me in ways I couldn't appreciate yet. He suggested an out-of-the-way camping spot. I thanked him and left the store.

WELDON, NC | Mile 103

Population 1,374 | Est. 1745

"I don't offer this to everyone but you seem like a good guy. You can sleep in the fenced-off area behind the station if you like. There's grass back there. I'd let you stay at my house, but I have a meeting with a lady friend of mine," said Bobo, the security guard at the BP station. He was a Black man of about sixty-five, with a cataract in one eye and a thick sponge of white hair. I took Bobo up on his offer. Ten minutes later he brought me a chili dog and an apple turnover from Hardee's. The back of the BP station smelled like rotting garbage. Small leeches covered my tent when I awoke.

The next morning I got more roadside prayers, this time from Shane. "May this man walk and bring pure peace to the world. Lord Jesus, we hope in your name that this man will bring inspiration to millions of people along his road to the Pacific. In your name we pray."

At one point in my life I was quite religious. I spent four of my five high-school years living above a garage in an attic apartment with my dad. We kept all of our things packed in metal milk crates we had stolen from the grocery store on night raids. We didn't like the idea that the living arrangement would be anything other than temporary, so we kept our clothes in the crates for a quick getaway.

I started using a phrase Dad had learned in AA: "No mistakes in God's world." We shot at raccoons, squirrels, and rats trapped in our wall. When we missed: "No mistakes in God's world." We were living in Hinsdale, one of the wealthiest suburbs around Chicago, but in an attic. Kids drove BMWs and Range Rovers to school while I scrounged for change in couch cushions for lunch money. I knew something about the way things really were. Or so I told myself. God's higher plan wasn't supposed to be understood.

After things started to improve financially for my dad, I asked him to send me to an all-boys' Opus Dei high school so I could play baseball. The team wasn't very good, and I knew they would play me. There, I started going to church daily. I took my Catholicism into the military, where I was nicknamed "the deacon" in basic training because I held Bible study grou[illegible] was permanently stationed in Fort Lewis, Washington, [illegible] much as I could: Thomas Merton, C. S. Lewis, Saint Au[illegible], Thomas Aquinas, John of the Cross, T. S. Eliot, W. H. Auden, and various Eastern mystics. I controlled the fear and pain of being locked down in a brutal simulated training mission or, later, in the middle of nowhere in Afghanistan, with the consolation that a better place was waiting for me and that someone was looking out for me. I highlighted nearly every word of a leather-bound St. James Bible. The squeaking sound of the highlighter was soothing. I usually read under a red headlamp on guard duty, when it was quietest.

Robert called across the street from inside his house: "Hey man, do you want something to drink?" "Sure," I said. I walked across the street to his modest house, which had Christmas decorations hanging from the front porch and a broken vacuum and shattered TV sitting next to the side door. A spotted mutt tied to a tree yapped in the backyard. Robert said, "Come in." I maneuvered my pack into the house. Robert was Black, about six-foot-six, and in his late thirties. "Man, I've been there." "Where are you coming from?" I told him as I filled my water bottle with ice and water from his fridge. I met his wife Jesse, who was white and in her late twenties; she was recovering from knee surgery. The exchange was brief, but it sat well with me the rest of the day. It was the first house I had entered in thirteen days. It is probably easier to offer help to a stranger if you can remember feeling like one yourself.

TWENTY MILES EAST OF RALEIGH, NC | Mile 165

Lowdog met me on the side of Highway 97, outside of Raleigh, with dinner. The GPS tracker on my backpack sent a signal of my exact location through Google Maps via my blog. The blog was usually mentioned in the interviews I did, so people could always figure out where I was. My mom loved this bit of technology: she watched an image of a small foot—me—inch its way across the US map for eight months. She said later, "As long as I could see that foot moving, I knew you were OK."

This was how Lowdog found me. He had spent the whole day in Raleigh so we could have dinner together. Lowdog received his call sign in the Patriot Guard Riders, a motorcycle group that escorts the funeral processions of fallen soldiers. He was in Raleigh for an interview, having lost his job in Norfolk the previous week. When he was eighteen, he told me, he had spent four days and four nights without food or water in the middle of a Texas desert. The "coyote" who was supposed to help him cross the border was arrested by the US Border Patrol and Lowdog was left to fend for himself. "My number-one hero and inspiration is Pat Tillman. I've read everything I could get my hands on about Pat," he told me. He had seen the interview Pat gave to ESPN before enlisting. "Here's a guy that has certain things in life: money, fame, school, and a beautiful wife, but he is striving to do even better. He is willing to put it all at risk in order for something more, something bigger than just him. So that got my attention and I started learning more about the guy. I did research." He had finished Mary Tillman's book a few days earlier, he said, adding that he tried every day to "bring something positive to the country I love so much, just the way Pat did."

RALEIGH, NC | Mile 185

Population 403,892 | Est. 1792

The first eleven miles of my road to Raleigh were easy. The last two required all of my willpower. The worst thing you can do when you are uncomfortable is to anticipate relief. I approached the hotel dreaming of a hot shower. Jim, a family friend from Chicago, had paid for my stay at the Hyatt. I felt like the boy raised by chimps when I checked in. I was dirty, breathing from my mouth, and staring openly at the luxury around me.

"Welcome to the Hyatt. Where are you coming from?"

"I'm coming from the forest," I said. The receptionist just stared. The porter reached for my pack; I grunted at him, grabbed it myself, and limped to my room in front of a lobby full of onlookers.

Google Maps' "walking" mode, via my BlackBerry, helped me leave Raleigh the next day. The technology was specific to foot travel, guiding me away from subdivisions with malfunctioning sprinkler systems and the like. My adventure felt safe, by Lewis and Clark standards.

In one of Raleigh's more affluent neighborhoods, a large maroon Chevy Suburban pulled up next to me. Inside were two well-dressed middle-aged women who seemed to be on their way to an open house, judging from the real-estate signs in the back seat. "We saw you walking and felt sorry for you. Do you take donations?" I was in fresh clothes, with a full stomach and a trimmed neckbeard, feeling sharp after staying at the Hyatt. Did I look that bad? With gas at $4.19 a gallon in Raleigh, I wanted to give *her* a donation when I saw all that maroon rolling down the street.

"Of course I accept donations! Thank you very much!"

"Good then, be safe and have a nice day."

I enlisted in the military soon after 9/11. The US response to 9/11 seemed to make sense; if we were attacked, then we should defend ourselves. But because I didn't think eighteen-year-old kids should be the ones dragged overseas to fight the war, I signed up. If a war was going to be fought, people who knew what they were getting into should fight it. People like me. (Or so I thought.)

I wanted to become a Ranger. *Black Hawk Down*, a movie about a famous Ranger battle in Somalia during the Clinton era (starring Hollywood badass Josh Hartnett), sealed the deal. Dave Matthews Band's "The Space Between" played over the movie trailer. I thought the song was complicated—like me. I was in a space between after college. So I signed over my life.

I entered the army as a specialist. By February 2002 I was polishing boots, learning to shoot, standing at regular attention, and trying to stay sane amid the monotony of basic training. I graduated from basic training, jump school, and the Ranger Indoctrination Program, or RIP. Being broken down was euphoric, in a way. I liked having my nerves deadened via physical punishment. Learning to absorb all types of pain was freedom. I earned the highest physical fitness score in my graduating RIP class. I entered the military overweight and watched the pounds melt off. I could soon see my abs; a fellow Ranger, noticing me in the shower, once said, "You could be a model." Books, TV, sports, and women were eliminated from our lives. Physical fitness became the only way for us to track our personal development—no other growth mattered. I could manage only needing to be good at push-ups, sit-ups, the two-mile run, shooting, road marching, and saying "yes."

My first tour in Afghanistan was spent mostly at Camp Wright in Asadabad—not one of the camps the Department of Defense air-conditioned at the time. It looked like a set from a space adventure movie. There was a tall, dusty, rock-strewn hill behind the camp. It was covered in small bushes that Afghan men and women spent hours digging up, one by one, for a pittance of firewood. This poverty was the most violent thing I saw during my first tour. It was hard watching these people dig and dig for whatever heat those twigs would eventually provide. It was even harder seeing them as a threat. I arrived just after the initial sweep against the Taliban by the Air Force and Special Forces in the months immediately following 9/11. Most Afghans were still trying to decide if we were friends or foes at the time. The camp never seemed like a safe staging spot; we could be attacked from the high ground. And the Taliban—at least that's what the chain of command called them—used the hill to fire rockets at our tents once every few weeks. My ears had never absorbed anything so loud and intimidating. The sound took the air out of my lungs and a hot waxy coating of fear filled the space between my cheeks. But I felt an obligation to breathe deep and feign calm, particularly when I saw my tough-acting squad leader jump out of his skin with anxiety. "Get down! No! Get to the bunker! *No! Just get down! Grab your weapons!*" he'd scream confusedly as he stumbled out of bed trying to put on his pants. (The attacks usually happened at night.)

I learned then that there are only two ranks in the military when being attacked—the composed and the frantic.

The Eleven Charlies were told to counter these attacks by shooting mortars. I was an Eleven Bravo, a regular infantryman. I carried a grenade launcher attached to an M-4, and never had visual targets to fire back at—which relieves me. When it came down to it I realized I didn't have it in me to kill. I knew I would be destroyed forever if I did. My previous experience with killing amounted to shooting one pheasant with a BB gun. Gutting the dead bird, feeling its warm flesh get cooler, made me want to vomit. Why I thought I could kill another human is still a mystery to me.

Why the military thought I should be a Ranger is also confusing.

Eleven Charlies were the mortar men; their blast radius was far less exacting and could be sent out from a much longer distance than from my weapon. The mortar fire was completely indiscriminate. No one knew what the rockets would hit: A small hut? Goats? Goat herders? Kids? Even the thought of hitting "the enemy" felt wrong.

Occasionally someone in another platoon or company would roll over an improvised explosive device (IED). We'd hear stories of legs and arms being blown off, people being cut in half. Back at Bagram Air Base we saw the twisted wreckage of Humvees and pickup trucks—wreckage was usually airlifted back to the base. Some of the guys would respond soberly; others would howl, "I can't wait to kill me some motherfucking haji!"

Most soldiers' deaths in Afghanistan that year involved helicopters. Afghanistan's high altitude and thin air were not compatible with safe helicopter rides. We lost seven guys from the Special Forces in a helicopter crash on my first tour. So these rides were often our biggest concern. We'd squeeze into Chinook transport helicopters with all our gear and no room to move. Each helicopter ride made us wonder if it would be our last. We'd hit a pocket of air, drop thirty feet, and clutch each other tight. We usually flew at night, blacked out and guided by infrared lights, but when we flew during the day we saw a primitive human landscape that starkly contrasted with our technologically advanced helicopters and weapons. Crops grew on terraces that look like giant stairs carved into the mountains. Hundreds, if not thousands, of people live in high-altitude villages nourished by the ledge planting system, chickens, and goats.

If we were sent on quick in-and-out missions, we flew in Blackhawks. We supported the Navy SEALs, Special Forces, and Delta Force on their raids. Most of these missions—in fact, all of mine—were rooted in bad intelligence. We'd be told that a Taliban member was in some village and we'd be sent to extract them. The SEALs would storm into a house while we waited in the front yard. They'd grab an unsuspecting guy along with any other males in the household, throw sandbags over their heads, and take them back to the base with us. Most, I imagine, were let go; others were surely sent to Guantánamo or the like. We often later found out that the person we had targeted in the extraction had been falsely accused by a neighbor after a squabble. We were rarely more than heavily armed, testosterone-filled pawns in village disputes.

The most notable mission I undertook for the US government was to jump into the tri-border area, where Afghanistan meets Pakistan and Iran. The rumor was that we landed in Iran—but that was never confirmed. The idea was to get people talking via satellite phones so we could intercept their calls. It worked. Forty-eight hours later, after we jumped into a desert that may or may not have been in Iran, the CIA captured Khalid Sheikh Mohammed, the guy whose photo with the long, frizzy bed-head and white V-neck T-shirt was all over the news, one of the supposed masterminds behind 9/11. All we did was jump out of a plane in the middle of night and lay in a prone position for twenty-four hours. This, apparently, was enough to get the phones running and reveal Mohammed's position. So we took credit for his arrest and got a bronze service star for the effort.

The Iraq war broke out in the middle of this tour. Once I returned from the end of my first tour, I started to realize that the mission in Iraq—in which I was now obligated to fight—was not what I had signed up for. The chain of command was hoping we'd just lump it in with Afghanistan in the "War on Terror." "Middle Easterners are all the same—religious fanatics. That region is basically one big country, isn't it?" I'd hear. But it became clear that the Iraq invasion was illegal according to the US Constitution.

Congress never declared war on Iraq. We were violating Article 1, Section 8 of the Constitution. But the Constitution wasn't something I obsessed over. I knew the law rarely applied to the people who held the real power and controlled the money. My big concern was that I now saw myself as an imperialist, a stormtrooper—someone who goes into another country to take other people's resources. There were too many US-supported dictators in the world—Hosni Mubarak in Egypt, King Abdullah in Saudi Arabia, and Moammar Gadhafi in Libya, to name a few—for me not to notice that the US only cared about the ones who decided against giving their oil to the West. I didn't want to kill anyone for oil. Killing someone who is trying to do you harm is unnatural enough. Killing someone so rich people can get richer was something entirely different. I didn't want to be an empire builder, a Roman soldier, like the person who killed Jesus. I couldn't square it in my mind.

TWENTY MILES WEST OF RALEIGH, NC | Mile 205

I noticed a long run of polished chrome beside the Iron Horse, a biker bar. I hadn't had a beer in two weeks. I walked in, ordered a Budweiser, and brought it to a corner table in the back. A giant American flag hung over my table, precariously close to a dartboard. White Christmas lights hung from the ceiling. I stared at a Class of 1980 high-school graduation photo above the jukebox. The bar was filled with thirty leather-clad bikers who smoked, laughed, wore leather, and shot pool. They all seemed to be watching me from the corners of their eyes. I drank half my beer. I started to feel like a turd, so I threw my pack on to leave. The guy everyone seemed to be buying beers for stopped me.

"Where you going? You're not walking across the country, are you?" he laughed.

"I am," I said, and turned around so he could read the vinyl sign I had affixed to my pack. He read it out loud. The entire bar stopped to listen, then exploded into a loud cheer. They reached into their pockets and gave me a collective donation "from the Iron Horse." I stuffed the cash into my pocket, grateful and dazed.

CHARLOTTE, NC | Mile 324

Population 731,424 | Est. 1768

As I walked into Charlotte, I heard a distinctive sound that brought me back to my childhood. My head was down. It was eight o'clock on a Sunday morning and I had not seen a car in an hour. The silence was broken by the sound of the horn from the "General Lee." I looked up and saw a school bus painted in a confederate flag to mimic the famous car from *The Dukes of Hazzard*. Twenty kids had their faces pressed up against the windows, waving. I forced myself to wave back.

Wanting to take it easy, I walked a few miles south and found a bookstore, one of the few public spaces where loitering is encouraged. I ate a bag of beef jerky and reread the battle royale scene in Ralph Ellison's *The Invisible Man* in a cozy leather chair. I was usually tired at the end of the day, but when I could find the time and energy to read, the characters and images jumped out at me more vividly than they ever had, regardless of what I was reading. It was like a lucid dream every time. This was one of the great surprises of the walk. Stepping back from TV and the frenetic pace of city life slowed me down enough to see how much my mind craved pictures and stories.

I camped beside ancient blue-green boulders outside of Charlotte. I could have found a denser, more concealed site, but I wanted to sleep next to them. I woke with the warm sun, nestled soundly in a fortified organic cathedral of peace and stillness. I built a fire, ate, read, and packed up my camp. I was walking by 10:30, feeling fresh blood in my joints and muscles. I was healthy and strong.

Fighting the KKK in Monroe, NC

I was only a few miles north of Monroe, where in 1957 Robert Williams, president of the local chapter of the NAACP, dug trenches to fight back against the KKK, which had been terrorizing his neighborhood. The Klan had been driving through Monroe in large car processions, shooting guns in the air, throwing rocks, and sounding horns in response to Williams's attempt to desegregate local pools. Black boys and girls who were banned from swimming in whites-only pools were drowning in rivers and swimming holes. Robert Williams decided he'd had enough of Jim Crow. As the KKK neared Monroe for another round of threats, Williams and other men from the area unloaded their weapons. The Klan quickly retreated. Not long after, Monroe officials made it illegal for the KKK to move in motorcades.

3

South Carolina

SOUTH CAROLINA BORDER | Mile 330

I met Dan riding a bike he "found lying in the street." He pulled up next to me and asked if I cared if he walked with me. Dan was six foot two, 220 pounds, with broad shoulders and a crew cut covering a blunted-cone head that resembled the chalk mounds in pool halls. He was wearing a five-day beard and a five-week mustache. He was riding/walking/hitchhiking to, "maybe," the Florida Keys, looking for a place to settle down for a year or two. Dan slept in a heavy down winter coat in the grass on the side of the road whenever he was tired, which was usually the mid-afternoon and early morning. He was a few years younger than me but looked older. He said he'd spent a year and a half locked up for things he hadn't done. The official word on one of the charges was "stalking." I peppered the first of our two hours together with exaggerated stories of my military training and hinted at a full arsenal of unnamed protective measures resting in my cargo pockets. I expected him to pull out a knife and stab me for the contents of my pack at any time.

"Grenades?" he asked. I didn't answer.

Dan faded in and out of stories like a TV with bad reception. Occasionally he would land on something interesting, like his hobby of carrying around binoculars to follow and watch detectives and police officers who sat sleeping in their cars or spent too much time at the donut house. He would then call in to report their on-the-job listlessness—his payback for a lifetime of unqualified harassment. His stories quickly became reruns, but I was still happy to have my first walking buddy in twenty-eight days. I surprised myself when I started to like and generally trust him. He was a nomad who "trusted in the cycles of nature." He believed that food would be there when he was hungry and that he would find safe sleep when he was tired. We crossed the South Carolina border together and told our stories to a silver-haired woman selling apples. She insisted on donating two "special hybrid Golden Delicious apples" to our adventures. We sat on a well-manicured lawn in front of an elegant limestone and slate mini-mall and ate our apples under a tempered midafternoon sun. A few miles later Dan's road took him south, toward his coveted coast; mine pointed west, toward a lot of road construction. I missed him for a few thousand feet.

GAFFNEY, SC | Mile 379

Population 12,414 | Est. 1897

A menacing black cloud hung over the sky in Gaffney, South Carolina, a blue-collar industrial town. I spent an hour walking straight toward it. It finally burst and streams of ureic Gaffney rain poured down. I hadn't showered in days so I didn't mind.

SPARTANBURG, SC | Mile 399

Population 180,786 | Est. 1831

In Spartanburg I caught the 4:10 p.m. screening of Oliver Stone's *W.* with Josh Brolin, intent on giving myself a full twenty-four hours' rest to celebrate one month on the road. I slept through nearly the whole film, nestled in a red velvet chair in the blissfully cool, empty theater. I headed to Target afterward for supplies, with no idea where I was going to sleep. There was a mousehole's worth of sun in the sky. All I could see were residential homes, two mini-malls, and streetlights. The daylight continued to die. Finally I spotted a sign that read "Three acres for sale." I was saved.

Under the red glow of my headlamp, I climbed over the rusty strands of a barbed-wire fence, using my staff to clear a place amidst the vines for my tent. I could still see streetlights. I could hear a Chihuahua yapping and a man ordering a woman to buy him a bottle of Olde English beer. I built a small fire and warmed a can of clam chowder, savoring the solitude. For the first time in a month it felt like a Sunday. I had walked hundreds of miles, more than I had ever walked in a month. But there was so much more walking to do. I was still thousands of miles from the Pacific Ocean. The next morning I'd have to pick up the forty-five-pound pack and keep going, not knowing whom I'd meet or what trouble I'd get into.

HISTORICAL EASTERN BOUNDARY LINE OF THE CHEROKEE NATION | Mile 417

I crossed the historical eastern boundary line of the Cherokee Nation the following day. The official sign sat between a McDonald's and an AutoZone.

I was eating in a yellow plastic booth at Waffle House when Chuck, a three-tour Vietnam and Marine Force Recon veteran, limped up to me with his crutch. He told me how much respect he had for Pat and all veterans, and suggested I distribute the weight better in my pack. Chuck stood six feet tall, with a Khe Sanh Veteran hat and fingers thick like his Southern accent. During the war he and his team, he explained, had been pinned under heavy mortar and artillery fire for more than two months. In the middle of this seventy-seven-day North Vietnamese attack, a twenty-two-inch mortar landed directly in front of him. Both of his buddies, to his left and his right, were sliced in half. Chuck walked away unscathed. He said he'd spent years trying to understand why the mortar seemed to curve around him and hit his friends.

Chuck was still patriotic; angry about the loss of his buddies, he blamed the Vietnamese. He didn't look like he was ready to be challenged. I don't know if it was anyone's place to challenge someone who has experienced such trauma. Two and half million Vietnamese were essentially burned to death by the United States in Chuck's war. How could anyone make peace with that?

When I met Pat Tillman I was in Ranger School. It was a Friday night and my class and I were on weekend leave at Fort Benning, Georgia. By then I was considering leaving the military, but I didn't know how. I was a good Ranger—on paper—and loved the camaraderie and challenge of the military. But Iraq felt like a bait-and-switch—and a betrayal. I took a cab to downtown Columbus, a town a few miles from Fort Benning. I was by myself because I always worked out a little extra after we were dismissed. The illusion of physical fitness as a deterrent against danger was what I clung to—that and my religion. I was on my way to meet a few guys at Scruffy Murphy's, an Irish bar. I walked passed Fountain City Coffee, the local coffeehouse, and noticed Pat and his brother Kevin chatting inside. We were in the same pre-Ranger class, but I had only met them briefly. I had stopped following sports in college, when I realized I wasn't going to become a professional basketball or baseball player, but had read an article about Pat in *People* magazine while on my first tour in Afghanistan. Beyond that, I knew little about him. I decided to walk in and say hi. Pat had a book in his hand and was drinking coffee with Kevin and another guy—a stark contrast to the drunken revelry no doubt already under way at Scruffy Murphy's. They invited me to have a seat. They were discussing religion.

I found myself defending the idea of God. "Doesn't the concept of something transcending matter, rather than matter always being around, make more sense?"

Pat and Kevin listened with an inquisitive and intense interest I rarely saw. Never did either act distracted or try to interrupt someone else's point to make his own.

Pat asked questions: "What created that which transcends matter?"

I tried to repeat what I'd memorized in college about Immanuel Kant. "Our five senses take in a certain amount of reality, but we can't presume it is the entire reality. Our finite senses are dealing with an infinite reality. Pointing to that unknowable reality is pointing to God," I said confidently.

"If something exists outside of our ability to comprehend it, what good is it? And what happens if this unknowable thing justifies behavior? Would you say that anything is allowed when the motivations for behavior originate in the unknowable?" Pat said.

From that moment on, Pat and Kevin were the only ones I wanted to hang out with during Ranger School. I would later learn from Kevin that he and Pat liked to read on a wide range of topics and then write papers to exchange with each other. They loved learning.

That night I was less interested in the content of the conversation than in the fact that I was having one that was triggering dormant parts of my brain. Critical thinking is considered effeminate and generally discouraged in the military. No one is going to follow an order into a machine-gun nest if they are used to stopping and thinking about things beforehand.

We closed the coffee shop and drove back to the base in a cab together.

TRAIL OF TEARS | Mile 430

Walking across the eastern US, sleeping on the ground, cooking with dried pine needles and twigs, and shaking the dirt out of my shoes after hours of walking helped me feel connected with the land. That sense faded as I walked through Pickens County, South Carolina, a vast estate acquired in a genocidal con: the step-off point of the "Trail of Tears."

I spent the rest of the day walking around Duke Energy, a nuclear energy facility hundreds, if not thousands, of acres in size. "Do Not Trespass" signs and iron-curtain fences surround it. An electric buzzing sound hung in the air. Three enormous reactors and a white water tower, adorned with giant hula hoops to create an atom effect, pierced the sky. The cold morning air and the heated water of Lake Keowee created an unnatural fog—like someone had dropped a boulder of dry ice in a swimming pool. I walked along the red clay beach between the skeletal power towers for what seemed like an eternity, and tried not to take deep breaths that day. *No mistakes in God's world.*

The Cherokee Nation

The Indian Removal Act passed Congress by five votes on May 28, 1830. The country was divided over the fate of Native Americans, with the South in favor of removal. The nation's first gold rush took place in Georgia in 1829. There was money to be made in the heart of Cherokee land.

The Cherokees tried desperately to Europeanize themselves. Many became carpenters, lawyers, and successful business owners. They created a written language. Nearly two thousand of them even owned slaves. But assimilation was not enough. It is estimated that that four thousand Cherokee people died on the nine-hundred-mile march at gunpoint to Oklahoma.

President Andrew Jackson responded to this news by asking, "What good man would prefer a country covered with forests and ranged by a few thousand savages to our extensive Republic, studded with cities towns, and prosperous farms, embellished with the improvements which art can devise or industry execute?"[3]

THIRTY MILES FROM THE GEORGIA BORDER

I could see the Appalachian Mountains. The leaves were finally turning yellow, plum, and a sweet fall red. The cold, thank goodness, takes its time in the South.

I walked a painful ten miles through rain and over more than a few hills to get to a forgettable Exxon gas station that served lunch. Pizza cut into large rectangles was spinning slowly in a glass box. It had been sitting under an orange light bulb for what looked like days. I bought three pieces and ate standing up as water dripped from the brim of my hat. A mile and two hills later, I realized I had forgotten my staff.

I hid my pack under a fallen log a few hundred feet into the forest on the side of the road and ran after my stick in the pouring rain. I would have run fifty miles to get it if I had to. I found it waiting for me in the men's room, next to a broken hand dryer.

The next morning I passed four miles of cattle ranches and farms as the sun tried to peer through a thick fog. I was still damp from the previous night's rain and my pack was heavy with wet gear. My goal was to walk into Walhalla—"garden of the gods"—to eat and find a coin laundry.

WALHALLA, SC | Mile 460

Population 3,801 | Est. 1849

At the Oconee Heritage Center I met Luther, who gave me a brief history of the town and county. We chatted, and I was off to the laundry. Afterward I headed to a café across the street. Colleen, the owner, was talking with Stewart, a pottery artist, when I walked in. Stewart and his girlfriend Sara were setting up a display of pottery. They invited me to stay the night. Three states into the walk, I was staying the night at a stranger's house.

Stewart's house rested on twenty-two acres that had been in his family since the 1850s. While we learned each other's life stories, he brought me behind the house and taught me how to toss throwing axes into a large stump of wood. Then he showed me a moss garden he had designed. It was buried deep in a dense patch of trees and outlined with geometric patterns and a compass made of stones, moss, bricks from the 1920s, and glass. Oil lamps were buried in the ground and nested in pottery sculptures. They illuminated patterned glass bottles, abstract driftwood sculptures, pottery, and his "wax resident moss-god." "I don't take many people back here," Stewart said. "But I thought you'd appreciate it." The moss-god was the most disturbingly beautiful piece of yard art I had ever seen: bones from dead animals, wax from melted candles, eyes made of glass bottles. But there was a humanity in it. It was clearly not the work of a psychopath. I thought about all the other Stewarts in the world I didn't know about.

We went next door to help Stewart's dad move a table. I stood in his parents' game room and saw the name Luther Lyle on a few plaques. The name sounded familiar. Luther came down stairs—it was the same Luther I'd met at the Oconee Heritage Center. He didn't look surprised to see me. "I figured I'd run into you again," he said. As the town historian, he'd recently finished a documentary about Native Americans in Oconee County. We went back to Stewart's house and watched the film on an old TV in the basement, which doubled as a pottery studio and classroom for little kids. Luther showed me the flag he had designed with the local Cherokee council. It was the same flag that hung on nearly every lamppost in Walhalla. It had the Cherokee symbols for land, water, and the red circle of life. Luther explained that *Oconee* means "land beside the waters," and the five rivers on the flag represented the Chattooga, Chauga, Keowee, Seneca and Tugaloo Rivers. He was proud of his design, and equally proud of his collaboration with the Cherokee.

I was off early the next morning. Stewart and I said we would stay in touch. Through no fault of either of us, that was the last time we spoke. I feel bad about that sometimes.

4

Georgia

CLAYTON, GA | Mile 487

Population 2,019 | Est. 1823

Jeff and Georgia asked me if I needed help. I said no, and they asked me where I was going.

"Clayton. I'm walking to California," I said.

I had not seen a car in an hour and a half when they pulled up. I saw only hemlocks, white oaks, mountain laurels, and a sloping unpaved dirt road. I heard the occasional bird chirp and felt a calm October morning breeze. I sat down for a rest, and a dark green pickup truck with a Forest Service sticker on the door panel pulled next to me. Jeff, a Forest Service ranger with blonde hair and in his mid-forties, replied, "Not on this road, unless you plan on swimming." I stood up and approached the passenger window.

"Well, what do you mean? The map says there's a road right here." I pointed to a clearly marked road on my fold-out map.

"This road runs into the Chattooga River."

"No bridge?"

"Nope."

"That explains why I haven't seen any cars this morning."

"Yep."

"How wide is the river?"

"Forty feet."

"Is there a road with a bridge on it anywhere around here?"

"Yeah, go back to the four-way stop sign and take Old Chattooga Road. It will take you south, though."

"I think I'll take my chances with the river, it's not that cold."

"Did you know I met a guy just like you about twenty years ago? I saw him sitting on the side of the road like you. I pulled over and asked him if he needed help, like I asked you. You know what he said?"

"What?"

"He said, 'I was waiting for you.' Can you believe that? He said he waited three hours in the same spot and prayed I would come. He ran out of water. You know what he called himself?"

"What?"

"Alex the Great. Can you believe that? He said he was walking across the country, but he'd started where you're trying to go."

"Wow."

"I never forgot him. He actually sent me a postcard when he got to Florida, thanking me for the water."

"That's a great story. Thanks for stopping. I look forward to conquering that river!"

I grabbed my staff and started down the road almost at a trot, imagining myself constructing an elaborate pulley system. I would cross the river without touching the water, I mused. At the very least my pack wouldn't touch the river. I'd use the hundred feet of parachute cord I carried with me, tie the end of it to a rock, and lasso a tree branch with it, then shuttle my pack and possibly myself across the river. The dirt road became a trail after two miles and the trail wound down to the river for another mile. The river was easily a hundred feet wide. I am not an expert at gauging distance, but it was certainly much wider than forty feet. It was also gorgeous. Rolling rapids, fall leaves, a soft, wheat-colored beach and a hundred feet of what looked like waist-deep water separated me from the state of Georgia.

It soon became clear that there would be no way to construct a pulley system. The distance was too great and there were no obvious branches sticking out over the water that I could do anything with. Instead I stripped down to the business end of my birthday suit, leaving my shirt and jacket on. I waterproofed my phone and camera, in case I went in. Then I threw my pack on and started to cross. The water felt like billions of fire ants attacking me at once. Thankfully, it only went three-quarters of the way up my thigh. I breathed deep, focusing on the other side. There was no turning back. My staff again proved to be a trusty sidekick. I would have slipped without it. I noticed thousands of flakes of pyrite, or "fools' gold," shimmering in the water. I made it across and smiled at the accomplishment. I was in the clear—and finally in Georgia.

I dressed quickly and realized, as I put on my socks, that my blisters were filled with river water.

After three-quarters of a mile I saw the forty feet of river the ranger had been talking about—only this branch of the river seemed to have no bottom. My heart huddled in fear in the back corner of my ribcage. Again, the pulley system wasn't an option. I shut down my nervous system as well as I could with deep meditative breathing. I stripped back down, taking off my shirt and jacket. I would carry my pack over my head. Naked, I entered the water. I began to lose feeling from my chest down.

Then the staff lodged itself between two hard rocks, slipped out of my hands, and began bouncing off rocks and driftwood. I doggy-paddled after it with one hand. All I could do was let my pack float downriver with me, trying to keep it from going under. I figured I had about thirty seconds before I would lose complete use of my limbs from the cold. I recovered the staff a hundred feet downstream, caught on a fallen tree. After making it to the other side, I sat down and had a sopping wet Cinnamon Toast Crunch cereal bar, staring at my wet pack. I thought of Alex the Great and wonder if he had similar difficulties. I felt like Rory the Average.

I climbed a very steep ridge. I wanted to be isolated for dinner.

I hung my wet clothes out to dry. I wanted to cry. I was a mess, inside and out. I tried to relax in the idyllic woods, but I was too embarrassed about how ready I had been to walk across the river naked. I could have slipped and never been heard from again. I was embarrassed about my mind, a mind that preferred being alone, naked and scared in a cold river, to working in a bank. How would I ever make a decent living again? How could I have a life that didn't regularly involve such dangerously fun small adventures?

Clinging to my wet sleeping bag, with a balled-up shirt as my pillow, I fell asleep. I woke up covered in dew, relieved but cold.

The next morning, I dragged myself out of the woods and plopped down into a booth at the Clayton Café for breakfast.

The restaurant was empty, but Laurie and her daughter Soleil chose the booth directly facing mine. "What are you doing?" Laurie said forcefully. We began to talk. We soon realized we had a mutual acquaintance, Colleen, the café owner in Walhalla. Soleil and her mom invited me back to their homestead for the night. There I met Laurie's ex-husband James, who was standing in the kitchen. Laurie let him come over whenever he wanted to visit the kids. After a few niceties he said, "Hey, did you know beans are just as good straight from the can? I never bother cooking them." He grabbed a can of beans from the cabinet, opened the can with his pocketknife and commenced eating. Then he said he had to go.

The house rested on two and a half acres overlooking Sumter National Forest. Laurie and her other daughter, Destiny, took me on a tour of the grounds—which included an expansive multi-crop organic garden, an authentic Sioux tipi with a chimney stove—which would be my home that evening—a huge trampoline, an outhouse, a treehouse, a fire pit, and a cedar hot tub, and we went inside to the wood-burning stove. Laurie wasn't rich, but she appeared to have it all, substituting creativity and resourcefulness for money. Most of the things in her backyard were built with found objects. Destiny, her adorable nine-year-old, was like her sister Soleil: self-confident and ready to talk. They were both homeschooled.

I offered to help around the house before dinner. I chopped wood, watered garlic rows, transplanted flowers, and covered basil plants with dark green tarps before a potential frost that evening. After a healthy garden-grown feast, the family invited friends over for a drum circle around a bonfire. Djembe drums, tambourines, flutes, and shakers emerged. It was the first time I had ever been asked to do anything like this. I had to fight the awkwardness brewing inside of me. I had to participate; it would be bad manners to not to join in. My hands, wrist, forearms, elbows, and shoulders wanted to seize up as I slapped the drums. I fought the rhythm, but I also fought fighting the rhythm. I looked up at Laurie; she had a hypnotized expression on her face, but when she saw me looking at her I froze. She smiled a knowing smile and mouthed the words "just let it happen."

"I knew you were breaking through a psychic wall," she said later.

I was surprised by how much I began to enjoy the sound of my hands slapping the animal skin. I began to feel fluid. I looked up again and saw Laurie's face lit by the flames and the silhouette of poplar trees swayed in the warm fall wind behind her. I was only interested in her opinion—she had an inner strength and confidence. I wanted to impress her. I learned a new form of communication that night: Who would be content to support the beat? Who would lead the next discussion? The rest of the night I felt content and assured under the Georgia firmament. Nothing felt rigid. I had traveled a long way from military formations and bank cubicles—hadn't I? We drummed for more than three hours as large slabs of wood were fed to a hot four- or five-foot fire.

That night the temperatures dropped to below freezing, but the space inside the tipi stayed warm. I had lucid animal dreams.

DICK'S CREEK GAP, APPALACHIAN TRAIL | Mile 503

Laurie offered me the tipi for the winter—it was tempting. I could have learned a lot. But I had to keep moving.

At five o'clock the next afternoon I walked onto the famous Appalachian Trail, also known as the People's Trail. I set up camp at Dick's Creek Gap. I could tell I was on the trail because of the white rectangle swatches that marked the trees. More than eighty-three thousand of these famous white markers show the way along the trail. The Appalachian Trail was completed at the end of the 1930s and some say it is the longest-running volunteer cleanup effort in the world. Ninety percent of the trail is maintained through donated labor. I was only a short distance from Springer Mountain, the official trailhead. The trail extends north 2,200 miles to Mount Katahdin in Maine. Every year, two thousand hikers attempt to "through-hike" the full length of the trail. Only a quarter make it. Along the trail you can see bears, bobcats, gray fox—there is even a herd of wild horses said to be roaming the second section of the trail in the Virginia highlands.

With November one day away, my campsite was well broken in. Stones encircled ash-filled fire pits, half a dozen long wood beams were propped on short, chubby logs for comfortable bench seating, and the ground was pressed flat from millions of hiker and animal steps. The well-worn trails, white painted squares, beautiful views, and quiet made me want to come back to the Appalachian Trail for a proper hike.

It was Halloween. A black bear tried to make things festive by walking a few feet from my tent. Laurie had reminded me to burn all remnants of food. The bear gave my site a few sniffs and was on his way. Whether the bear thought so or not, I felt like part of the landscape by then—like a fallen log. I was surprised that I wasn't more frightened. Maybe I was just too tired to imagine what it would be like to be eaten by a bear. The military taught my brain to ward off images of my demise. I wouldn't have done half the things I did in the military if I was good at envisioning my death. I was still living out my training to be a bullet stopper. I played with the long bracelet Laurie had given me before I left.

BLUE RIDGE, GA | Mile 553

Population 1,290 | Est. 1886

I walked for seventeen miles without seeing a house or store. My beard was two weeks old: I hadn't shaved since Spartanburg. It was starting to look like the parched highway ditch grass I was spending so much time on. I had dreams that the beard was gathering old lotto tickets, cans of Sparks—sort of a cross between Red Bull and malt liquor—and decomposing raccoon jaws.

I earned my food that day. On one hill the asphalt was so steep it nearly touched my nose. I spent a half hour getting to the top. I was expecting my line of sight to fall off the curve of the earth at the summit. Instead my eyes bored a hole into the base of many bigger mountains fifty miles away. I'd thought I was making good time through the Appalachians. Now I wasn't sure I had left the foothills. But I kept going.

The next day the sky was bright with stars, satellites, and a lemon-wedge moon. As I was climbing to the top of a hill I noticed a dirt-colored, whipped mound of a kind I had not seen since my time in Montana, where my dad lived: bear droppings. Eating my dinner on a fallen pine tree fifteen minutes later, I looked up and saw a large black bear twenty-five feet from me. His black-tire head, brown-axle nose, and disappointed dark eyes looked at me as if to say, "I walked all the way up here for ramen noodles?"

We stared at each other for a while. I was paralyzed. My legs felt dead. I was shocked when an image of him disemboweling me on the mountain flashed before my eyes. He could have had his way with me. I untied the strap Laurie gave me, which kept my staff fastened to my pack. Then I tried to slowly reach into my bag to grab my camera, my hands shaking as I fished around in the pack. He ran down the hill before my hand emerged with the camera. I could've sworn I heard him grunting, "No food, no picture."

ELLIJAY, GA | Mile 568

Population 1,619 | Est. 1834

I camped on a bluff, staring east at the mountain where I'd met the bear the previous evening. The sun rose and ignited the leaves in the valley below. It was a sunrise that demanded every bit of my attention. There was no stretching, packing, eating, or even breathing.

I hiked for three hours at a steep incline to the top of a big hill outside the Chattahoochee-Oconee National Forest to be interviewed on NFL Radio. It was my highest point yet in the Appalachians. I could see a hundred miles to the northeast from the top. I set up camp in a thick bed of crunchy yellow leaves and realized I'd set up my tent under a mansion. There seemed to be no movement in or around it, so I stumbled up a slope littered with deadfall to investigate. The porch of the house shot over a cliff into the purple north Georgia sky. There were two rocking chairs. The rest of the house was sealed, with a "For Sale" sign in the front graveled driveway. I took a seat in one of the chairs, charged my phone from an outdoor electrical outlet on the deck, and waited for my interview to begin. Media outlets were reaching out to me at that point; my blog was getting between seven and fifteen thousand hits a day. My interviews were as apolitical as I could make them—I was hoping to appeal to the largest possible audience. I talked about Pat's example and how we needed more leaders who could make decisions like Pat's if we were going to bring balance to the country. I always appealed for donations and repeated the Foundation mission statement:

> Family and friends created the Pat Tillman Foundation in 2004 to honor Pat's legacy and pay tribute to his commitment to leadership and service. The mission of the Pat Tillman Foundation is to invest in military veterans and their spouses through educational scholarships—building a diverse community of leaders committed to service to others.

Then I talked about the walk: the bears, the wonderful people I was meeting, and the joy I was experiencing as I tried to carry on Pat's example. The interviews went well. I was a feel-good story. I said nothing controversial. I was inspiring.

I made sure there was no trace of my visit before I headed back down to my tent.

That night I was asleep by 11:15. At 12:30, a noise put me on edge. I stepped out of my tent, looked around, and heard a few phlegm-filled barks. I instinctively woofed back and hit my staff on a rock. Six green eyes shone in the white beam of my headlamp. I was face to face with the canine version of John Steinbeck's Joad family. The dogs were out wandering the mountain, looking for odd jobs and a future. They looked like they had been traveling for days, hoping the Appalachians would provide them with stability in tough economic times—the stock market had fallen almost a thousand points since my walk began. I assumed these guys were part of the fallout. My heart went out to them. I was tempted to call them over with a smooching sound and share some potato soup, but before I could they all ran down the mountain. I turned on "Dust Bowl Blues" by Woody Guthrie:

> These dusty blues are the dustiest ones I know,
> These dusty blues are the dustiest ones I know,
> Buried head over heels in the black old dust,
> I had to pack up and go.
> An' I just blowed in, an' I'll soon blow out again.

I Am Troy Davis

As I approached the Georgia line, a forty-year-old Black man by the name of Troy Anthony Davis was entering death watch in a maximum-security prison in Atlanta. For the third time in sixteen years, Troy Davis was on death row feeling what it was like to count what could have been the final hours of his life. Troy's execution date was set for October 27, 2008. Activists from around the world rallied for him that week. Amnesty International held twenty-five "Free Troy Davis" events.

In Savannah, that same week, Martina Davis-Correia prepared a suitcase for what she thought would be her final visit with her brother Troy. Martina had been spending nearly all of her time organizing support for Troy. The *New York Times*, the *Washington Post*, NPR, *Democracy Now!*, and the *Atlanta Journal-Constitution* had all covered the case because of Martina's unrelenting quest to prove Troy's innocence. Troy and Martina were only a year apart in age and were best friends.

Martina was also engaged in what would be a ten-year fight with breast cancer. She was a veteran of Operation Desert Shield. Her cancer was most likely a byproduct of her time in the military and of Gulf War syndrome—there was no other reported cancer in her family. As Martina clicked the clasps of her suitcase she heard her mother Virginia scream from the other room: "Praise God! The execution was stopped."[4] The date was October 24, 2008.

Troy was convicted of killing Mark MacPhail, an off-duty police officer in the early morning hours of August 19, 1989, outside a Burger King. There was no DNA evidence tying Troy to the murder and the gun used in the murder was never found. Troy's conviction hinged upon the testimony of nine supposed eyewitnesses, seven of whom later recanted, citing heavy police coercion to provide testimony against Troy. Some of the witnesses who recanted pointed the finger at Sylvester "Redd" Coles, one of the two witnesses who didn't recant, and the only person at the scene of the crime who admitted carrying a gun the night MacPhail was killed.

Two years later, on September 21, 2011, Troy found himself strapped to a gurney for three hours as he waited for word on a fourth stay of execution. Troy was the top news story in the country the day the Supreme Court rejected the final appeal in his case. He would not get off the gurney that night. The dissenting decision from the Supreme Court amounted to admitting that, yes, there is evidence that Troy is innocent. But the Supreme Court can't stop an execution because there has been a fair and full trial.[5] As Martina used to say, "The system doesn't care whether Troy is innocent or not, just whether legal procedures were followed correctly."[6]

People including Desmond Tutu, John Lewis, former FBI director and judge William Sessions, Jimmy Carter, and Pope Benedict XVI all called for the release of Troy Davis, but Georgia's justice system could not admit that it had held an innocent Black man on death row for nearly twenty years. Troy's execution via lethal injection was carried out at 11:08 p.m. on September 21, 2011; millions of people from around the world, including me, wretched in horror as it was announced that Troy had been killed. It felt like a state-sanctioned lynching to many of us. A white police officer had been murdered and a Black man would pay for it—and it didn't matter which Black man it was. Martina died of complications from breast cancer two months to the day after Troy was executed. Troy left his supporters with these final words in a letter he wrote shortly before his death:

> There are so many more Troy Davis'. This fight to end the death penalty is not won or lost through me but through our strength to move forward and save every innocent person in captivity around the globe. We need to dismantle this unjust system city by city, state by state and country by country.
>
> I can't wait to Stand with you, no matter if that is in physical or spiritual form, I will one day be announcing, "I AM TROY DAVIS, and I AM FREE!"

CHATSWORTH, GA | Mile 592

Population 4,299 | Est. 1832

I stepped in a pothole and twisted my ankle outside of Chatsworth. Limping, I relied on my staff a little extra that day.

Chatsworth is seventy-four miles northwest of Dahlonega, Georgia, the home of the "mountain" phase of Ranger School. I never made it past the initial phase in Fort Benning, Georgia. It was a lesson in sleep and food deprivation. I thrived on the experience in many ways. Without food or sleep, you start finding new pockets of reserve energy in your body. I was fascinated by this. Before joining the military, a day after I finished the book *Black Elk Speaks,* I tried to spend twenty-four hours in the woods of Montana without food or water to see if I could experience anything interesting. It lasted about eighteen hours before I walked home and devoured a box of Special K cereal and two Budweisers.

In the first phase of Ranger School I dropped a radio during a patrol exercise and had to spend two hours looking for it while the instructors followed me with crossed arms and taunts. It was cause for a "recycle," meaning I would have to redo that phase. This was a common thing in Ranger School, but I was stunned; I remember fighting off tears. Pat Tillman put his hand on my shoulder after I walked out of the instructor's office with the news and told me he remembered how embarrassed he was riding the bench as a rookie with the Arizona Cardinals. He told me to stick it out.

Waiting for the second phase to begin gave me a lot of time to think about what the military was asking of me. I consumed massive amounts of food trying to recover the nutrients my body had been denied. I was confined to a room full of bunk beds and had limited range, outside of the bunks, an attached TV room, and the Ranger School cafeteria. I felt like a little kid who was grounded for bad grades, with a Ranger School instructor/babysitter occasionally coming by to check in on me. The prospect of not finishing the class with Kevin and Pat also bothered me. They were steady and irreverent.

Ranger School was a mind-erase, a reprogramming exercise, a rite of passage. I'd be a more confident soldier when it was done. I'd be more confident in the presence of the soldiers I would lead and take orders from. I'd be more confident carrying out the mission.

I had just spent nine months intimidating poor people in Afghanistan, a country that may or may not have contained the guy who may or may not have been responsible for the 9/11 attacks. I remembered the young children who stared as we carried heavy weapons through their villages, the men we took from their homes, and the women who watched in horror. I thought about those who had been on the receiving end of our mortar rounds and air strikes. Surely innocent people were just as likely to be hit as the men who shot rockets at us. But why were they shooting rockets at us in the first place? Were they just defending their homes? Men stood in front of their clay homes in some of the most primitive and impoverished villages on earth, forced to grin as Humvees, machine guns, and bombs rolled down their streets. Any signs of disapproval and they'd be subject to the violent whims of the most militarily and technologically advanced country in history. Maybe I was too soft for the military. Maybe I didn't want to lose my heart and kill someone for a cause about which I now felt conflicted.

Maybe I didn't want to die or lose my mind. During those two weeks I began to convince myself that it was time to leave.

If I graduated from Ranger School, I'd be forced to lead other men back into Afghanistan or Iraq. Once you get your Ranger tab you're in charge of people. You have to make sure others kill. What is it like to tell others to kill for a cause you don't believe in? If I hadn't already been on a tour in Afghanistan, I probably wouldn't have quit. But I had been. If I had finished, it would have been much more difficult to find a similar opening. I was sure of one thing sitting in that holdover space in Ranger School: I wasn't bringing freedom and democracy to anyone. And as far as I could tell I wasn't making the United States safer for civilians back home.

I had seen enough. I was terrified by what that would mean. After two weeks of thinking and working up the courage, I walked up to a Ranger School instructor and said, "I don't believe in what I am doing anymore. I want out."

I had a good physical fitness record. I had been to Afghanistan. I was from Ranger Battalion, and next to no one from Ranger Battalion left Ranger School. The instructors almost pleaded with me to stick with it. Then they tried to shame me into continuing. "You're going to regret this the rest of your life"—I heard that at least a dozen times. I was soon put on a plane and sent back to Fort Lewis.

CHATTANOOGA, TN | Mile 635

Population 167,674 | Est. 1839

Tennessee was my fifth state line. Gas was $1.98. It was Veterans Day. I tried to focus on my understanding of freedom. That day, I sewed the second big rip that ran through the seat of my pants—preserving something I would have thrown out a few months prior.

I climbed Lookout Mountain, site of the third and final battle of Chattanooga during the Civil War in 1863. The third battle lasted three days in late November. The Confederate Army held what some considered an unassailable position on Missionary Ridge at the top of the mountain. Union troops, led by Major General William Sherman, defeated one of the South's two major armies and took Chattanooga, which was considered "gateway to the South." Four states were visible from the top of Missionary Ridge. Nearly six thousand were lost on the Union side. Six thousand six hundred Confederates died. Looking out, I tried to imagine the carnage that once littered the side of the ridge and the bottom of the hill, which was now blanketed by a subdivision. I couldn't.

Conscientious Objectors in the Civil War?

It is estimated that only 15 to 20 percent of all the soldiers in the Civil War actually fired their weapons when given the chance in battle.[7] That means 80 to 85 percent of all infantrymen in the Civil War were conscientious objectors at the critical moment when they stood face to face with the enemy in battle. This percentage remains consistent through World Wars I and II. The majority of the killing in these wars was done by artillerymen, who could inflict the most damage to the greatest number of people from the farthest distance, with the least possible personal interaction with those on the receiving end of their weapon. Lieutenant Colonel

Dave Grossman, in his book *On Killing*, points out that 90 percent of the 27,574 muskets recovered from the battlefield at Gettysburg were loaded.[8] Twelve thousand had been loaded more than once. Grossman, whose book began as an attempt to write a manual to improve the US military's ability to train its soldiers, came to the conclusion that the men holding the loaded weapons were willing to die before they killed other men. The muskets that were loaded multiple times were the result of soldiers posturing in front of authority and peers to give the illusion that they were fighting the enemy. Grossman goes on to say, "If most soldiers were desperately trying to kill as quickly and efficiently as they could, then 95% should have been shot with an empty weapon in their hand, and any loaded, cocked, and primed weapon available dropped on the battlefield would have been snatched up from wounded or dead comrades and fired." Most healthy humans, when they can see the whites in the eyes of the people they are supposed to kill, can't kill. I feel a tremendous empathy now for the men who died on Lookout Mountain, knowing that if I was one of them, I most likely would have been part of the majority who died with loaded weapons in their hands.

TRENTON, GA | Mile 654

Population 1,942 | Est. 1845

The next day I walked for distance. My personal best in one day was thirty-four miles. I asked people via my blog to donate one dollar for every mile I walked over thirty. I turned on my GPS so people could track me online. I headed out for the challenge at 2:44

in the morning. I left from 12629 Main Street in Trenton, Georgia, and ended the day with 38.1 more miles on my shoes.

Alabama is zoned like a game of fifty-two-card pickup, so sometimes it was hard to stay on course. I often walked east when I should have walked west. Fifty miles in one day was my goal. I remember being told in the military that, during WWII, the first paratroopers from the 101st were expected to walk 150 miles in three days. That number kept me humble.

After the challenge walk I woke up to a drum roll of rain on my tent roof. The temperature had dropped overnight. Unzipping my sleeping bag was like taking off a space suit on the dark side of the moon.

5

Alabama and Mississippi

SCOTTSBORO, AL | Mile 694

Population 14,770 | Est. 1870

Angie was my waitress at the Triple R BBQ. I was starving and she was quick to take my order. Eating real food instead of meals out of a can was deeply satisfying: the soul knows the difference between fresh Southern banana cream pie and strawberry powder mix filled with preservatives. There is hope in real food.

When I was finished, she asked about my walking stick and pack. She started to cry when I told the story. Then she told me about her victory over cancer. She pulled out a Saint Christopher medal that she wore every day. She said, "You need this now. I'd be honored if you carried this with you on your journey. It helped me get through my health problems." I did.

Jim Polk, a sixty-year-old man, had no idea why I was jogging down Highway 72 outside of Scottsboro at 9:30 in the morning. I was singing an improvised song about the Huddle House (it's like the Waffle House, but with red booths instead of yellow), which was my next destination and was now within eyeshot. My pack felt light. Jim was walking into McDonald's and called me from across the highway. "Come on over here and get yourself something to eat." I ran over and introduced myself and thanked him for the generous and courageous offer—I say courageous because I wouldn't have done it. I'm sure I looked like a lunatic. We walked into McDonald's and I said, "The people of Alabama sure have looked out for me! I've met quite a few beautiful people in the last forty-eight hours." The four people standing in line and the three ladies at the registers lifted their heads and smiled. "We *are* beautiful, aren't we?" said one of the ladies behind the counter.

Jim said, "Let me tell you a true story. I played basketball in high school and the only way I could get home from practice was to walk. No bus would stay that late and take me the five miles from the school to our farm. When I got home I would have to feed the animals. So when I see people walking, I make sure I help them the best I can."

I said, "Till this day you remember what it was like to walk all those nights after practice?"

"Yep."

He turned me around and read my sign. "Sure I heard of Pat Tillman. I coach and teach at the high school and have a lot of respect for what he did. I myself spent two years in Vietnam, sixty-seven to sixty-nine, in light infantry. Get this guy anything he wants and I'll have hot cakes and a sausage biscuit to go." Jim put fifteen dollars in my hand as he walked out the door. By that time I had raised ten thousand dollars for the Pat Tillman Foundation.

Lighting a fire after twenty-four hours of on-and-off rain was a good moment that day. Dry pine needles are best found hanging in the branches of healthy trees—look up, not down, to build a fire after rain. Footsteps woke me the next morning. My first thought was a deer—but the force behind the snapping twigs and crumpling leaves sounded like boots.

"This is private property."

I unzipped my tent to see a man with a shotgun standing over me wearing a full blonde beard to his chest and head-to-toe camo. Calmly I replied with foggy eyes and a dry mouth, "I'm sorry. It was dark when I set up camp and I didn't notice any signs. I'm on a cross-country walk."

"That's okay" was all he said, and he walked off. I pulled my head inside the tent and sat upright, deciding whether to lie down or pack up.

Looking back, I wonder: if I had been Black instead of white, would I have been shot? Would a Black man walking across the country sleeping on private property have had the same treatment? If I was in Florida, he could have shot me and said he was "standing his ground" on his private property. And if I was Black he most certainly would have been found innocent.

I heard footsteps once more. The man came back to my tent: "Hey, do you want this? It's an MRE. One of those military meals."

The night before, I had been looking forward to a strawberry-shake MRE packet—the last of the ten I had carried since the Atlantic. The powdery strawberry mix required only a bit of water and was something I saved for nights when I was far from towns. I searched my pack and was disappointed when I couldn't find it.

"Yes, that would be great. Thank you!"

He gave it to me and left without saying a word. That day I walked sixteen miles and didn't see one store or restaurant. I had food, but I would have had to boil water and use one of my expensive dried meals. The quiet man with the shotgun had saved the day.

The Scottsboro Boys

It's hard to enter Scottsboro without thinking of the Scottsboro Boys. In 1931, during the height of the Depression, nine young Black men ages thirteen to twenty-one were falsely accused of raping two white women. They had scuffled on a freight train with a group of white kids. They were all looking for work. The whites lost the fight and reported the incident to the stationmaster. The nine Black youths were arrested. When it was found that two white women were also on the train, the police charged the boys with rape, despite a complete lack of physical evidence to support the charges. A mob of Scottsboro residents stormed over to the jail where the boys were held and attempted to lynch them. The National Guard held the residents at bay.

After two weeks, an all-white jury found the defendants guilty. They were sentenced to death. Lawyers from the Communist Party petitioned for an appeal. The Alabama Supreme Court upheld the decision. The case was sent to the US Supreme Court where, following widespread protest, the court ordered the boys to be retried in Alabama. Ruby Bates, one of the alleged victims, wrote a letter to the *Daily Worker* saying that the boys had never touched her and that the police had forced her to lie.

In the fifth trial, four of the jailed were found innocent. The rest received sentences ranging from seventy-five years to life. It wasn't until 1950, nineteen years after they were arrested, that all the defendants were set free.[9]

HUNTSVILLE, AL | Mile 734

Population 180,105 | Est. 1811

The next day a cop pulled over and asked if I'd had words with an old woman after she caught me sleeping in her barn. I said, "No, officer. I slept off of Highway 72."

"Where are you from and who did you talk to today?"

"Chicago, and I spoke with two guys and a girl who pulled over in a red car and gave me some creamed canned corn. I also spoke to an older gentleman who stopped and asked me what I was doing walking these back roads. He was driving a car like that one." I pointed to the blue late-nineties Lincoln Town Car pulling up next to the patrol car.

A woman in her early seventies stepped out, walked toward me, and interrupted the officer. She hugged me and said, "My name is Shirley and my husband told me what you are doing. I wanted to bring you this." It was a stuffed monkey with a laminated picture of a man in his late twenties.

"This is my son," she said. "He was murdered nineteen years ago. I want you to take this with you. He was a ventriloquist, and he loved to tease the girls with this monkey. I think what you are doing is so good. My son enjoyed travel and I know he would love what you're doing as well." She handed the confused officer a camera and asked, "Will you take a picture of this handsome gentleman and me?" The officer fumbled with the camera for a few minutes and I showed him how to work it. In the meantime two other squad cars pulled up. Shirley and the new officers were on a first-name basis. There were no more questions about the barn.

When I entered Huntsville, the mayor's chief of staff, Trent Willis, picked me up and took me to Liberty Middle School, where Principal Sally Bruer greeted us. My cousin Cord had called the mayor the day before, told him I was coming to town, and suggested a speaking engagement. An assembly of two hundred middle-schoolers attentively listened as I talked of Pat's example, his love of learning, and the walk. I emphasized the importance of a person figuring out what they love to do and giving it away to the world.

"Are you scared?" asked one young boy.

"On some level I'm sure I am, but I'm good at blocking it out."

"What did you name your walking stick?" asked a girl with a University of Alabama sweatshirt.

"I haven't named it. Do you have any ideas?"

"Nooooo."

The kids came down from their seats to give me dollars and hugs as they left the gym.

After the assembly I went to the mayor's office and held a full press conference. For a brief second I thought about mentioning my exit from the military. Maybe I would say a few words about the unjust wars overseas and why kids should not be made to fight them. But I was nervous and shy. Besides, this walk was about raising money for the Foundation—I had to respect that. Or at least that is how I justified it to myself. Far-left views would surely alienate me from more than half the country. I couldn't risk that with so many more miles to go. It would be a few more states before I reconsidered the idea.

I received the key to the city and a new pair of shoes from newly elected mayor Tommy Battle. Quiet nights under the stars, shotguns in my face, encounters with wary police officers . . . then lights, news cameras, and a key to the city, all in the span of forty-eight hours. It was a dramatic contrast that gave me plenty to think about when I walked out of town. I imagined the same thing happening all across the country. Maybe I *could* raise 3.6 million dollars. My mind raced with hope and enthusiasm for what would come later. The press's questions weren't too different from those of the middle-schoolers. Then Mayor Battle, Councilwoman Sandra Moon, and I had a talk about what it takes to inspire people to do good. We agreed that people are motivated by actions, not words. Pat Tillman didn't talk about doing something that went against the grain of what was easy or comfortable for a greater cause. He just did it. The mayor and the councilwoman both wrote generous checks to the Foundation before I left City Hall.

Crossing a street on Highway 72, I saw a green Jeep with Auburn Tigers stickers on the door panels waiting at a red light. The woman in the driver's seat called me over.

"My husband and I saw you at a McDonald's in Scottsboro. We also saw you on the news yesterday and I drove around today hoping to run into you. I said to my husband, 'If God wants it to be, it will be.' I can't believe it! Would you like to come over for dinner?"

I wanted to knock out another five miles, but it was close to five p.m. already. I could have walked across the country in three months if I never spoke to anyone, but I would have missed so much—after all, "no mistakes in God's world."

Linda seemed surprised that I said yes. We drove to a beautiful house in Madison County, where I met her three dogs and her husband, a pastor named Darwin. The Serenity Prayer hung in the kitchen by the stove.

Darwin noticed me looking at the framed, handwritten words and said, "I work with young adults who have addiction problems."

"That's wonderful. I'm familiar with the prayer." I said.

Darwin nodded and we sat down to eat lasagna. The dogs got the scraps. Darwin and Linda asked me if I wanted to spend the night. A warm bed would have been wonderful, but I felt an inexplicable need to leave. Darwin dropped me off where Linda had picked me up and gave a generous donation.

At least ten cars had pulled over to donate that day. I walked for another hour in the dark.

FLORENCE, AL | Mile 802

Population 39,319 | Est. 1826

Paige's husband stepped out of the car and opened the side door, and I saw two boys and a girl between the ages of six and nine. "We knew it was you from the news when we saw your staff. My husband," she said, motioning to the driver's seat, "is a high-school history teacher and I teach special ed." The two boys knew who Pat was from a *Sports Illustrated* article titled "Remember His Name." They all got out to take a picture with me. Paige said, "Will you be walking during Christmas?" I said yes.

"Did you hear that, guys? Santa won't be bringing him any presents this year. So we are going to think a lot about Pat's decision and the reason why Rory will be away from his family this year." One of the boys handed me his Obi-Wan Kenobi toy and said, "I hope you get home soon." They thanked me and were on their way. I carried the toy with me for the rest of the journey.

I felt like I was swimming across the country that day. The rain was heavy and constant as I made my way to working-class Florence, home of the storied University of North Alabama football team, Tim McGraw, and Faith Hill—more than a few Florence residents reminded me of the latter two.

I arrived at City Hall and met Mayor Irons. I had begun calling mayors of the towns the day before I would be arriving. Organizing a talk in front of a school is much easier if the mayor does it for you. Principals and coaches would greet me and say, "The mayor's office just told us that a guy who served in the military is walking across the country and wants to talk about the Pat Tillman Foundation. Is there anything else I should know?" Pat Tillman's name was responsible for most of the ease with which these conversations occurred. People wanted to claim Pat Tillman as their own. Everyone wanted to be connected to his life in some way.

Mayor Iron's office arranged for me to speak to the University of North Alabama football team before practice and gave me the key to the city. I received five keys to five different cities across the

US before the walk concluded; it was always a thrill. At the Florence firehouse, eight firefighters had a spaghetti dinner waiting for me. A.J., a firefighter, showed me around the station; Captain Ezell and Chief Willett helped me plot my route. Battalion Chief Willett called the vice-president of the International Association of Fire Fighters union in Memphis to lay the groundwork for me to stay at a string of firehouses across the country.

The next day I spent eight hours listening to the slow, mile-consuming clap of my staff hitting pavement as a cold wind rolled over miles of exhausted cotton fields on County Highway 2. I saw only a handful of cars, one of which was driven by Captain Ezell from the Florence fire department. He pulled over to say hi and to check on me. I was cutting through the back country on a path decided on at dinner at the fire station. If there is a group of people you can count on for precise and efficient directions out of town, it is firefighters.

It was Thanksgiving. After pushing myself extra hard all day, I walked into Ryan's Buffet at five-thirty, hungry and cranky. I finished my first plate of turkey and dressing and was soon back to normal.

As I was leaving, Julia, a waitress not assigned to my table, grabbed my arm as I was negotiating my way around the crowded dining room and said, "I can see in your eyes you are doing important work. Stay on your path." She reached into her pocket and grabbed what seemed to be all of her tips from the evening and tried to give them to me. I refused four times as she followed me out of the restaurant. She finally grabbed me with a firm hand and said, "Continue to do what you are doing." And she pushed the money into my hand.

Ida B. Wells

Ida Bell Wells was born into slavery in Holly Springs, Mississippi, in 1862, a few miles south of Highway 72 where I walked.

By the age of sixteen Ida was working as a teacher to support her five siblings, after both her parents died from yellow fever following the Civil War.

In 1884, when Ida was twenty-one, she refused to move to the Black section of a train. She had to be forcefully removed:

> The moment he caught hold of my arm I fastened my teeth on the back of his hand. I had braced my feet against the seat in front and was holding to the back and as he had already been badly bitten, he didn't try it again by himself. He went forward and got the baggageman and another man to help him and of course they succeeded in dragging me out.
>
> They were encouraged to do this by the attitude of the white ladies and gentlemen in the car; some of them even stood on the seats so that they could get a good view and continued applauding the conductor for his brave stand.[10]

At the time, land and business owners in the South were fiercely resisting Reconstruction. The bosses wanted to keep whites and blacks divided by racism. If blacks were getting paid less because of racism then whites would have to compete against lower-wage workers, which would drive all wages down—increasing profits and power for the owners.

Lynching became endemic once Northern troops were withdrawn from the South. Wells estimated that more than ten thousand African Americans were lynched in the South between the end of the Civil War and 1895.[11]

Wells started documenting the nightmare of lynching in pamphlets. Frederick Douglass wrote her a letter after reading one of her pamphlets, *The Red Record: Tabulated Statistics* and *Alleged Causes of Lynching in the United States*. In the letter, Douglass said:

> If American moral sensibility were not hardened by persistent infliction of outrage and crime against colored people, a scream of horror, shame, and indignation would rise to Heaven wherever your pamphlet shall be read. But alas! Even crime has power to reproduce itself and create conditions favorable to its own existence.[12]

Whites fabricated many stories to justify the lynching of Black men, women, and children; amongst them were: rioting, insurrection, but rape was the primary lie told by whites before the lynching of Black men. As Wells explained:

> The Southern white man would not consider that the Negro had any right which a white man was bound to respect, and the idea of a republican form of government in the Southern states grew into general contempt. It was maintained that "This is a white man's government," and regardless of numbers the white man should rule.
>
> The government which had made the Negro a citizen found itself unable to protect him. It gave him the right to vote, but denied him the protection which should have maintained that right.[13]

CORINTH, MISSISSIPPI | Mile 860

Population 14,784 | Est. 1853

I jogged into Mississippi, the birthplace of William Faulkner and Richard Wright, my seventh state. Faulkner wrote, "To understand the world, you must first understand a place like Mississippi." Walk along the impoverished roads of DeSoto County just east of Memphis and you'll see what he meant. Run-down shacks, cracked pavement and sidewalks, and a lot of empty storefronts everywhere I turned. At 22.6 percent—35 percent for African Americans—Mississippi has the highest proportion of residents living below the poverty line in the United States.[14]

The sun set and the only light I saw was the extraterrestrial green flicker of the GPS tracker tied to my pack. Walking day in and day out for such an extended period of time often caused me to lose my mental coordinates. Certain regions of my brain shut down and others opened up. I crossed the mile-wide Tennessee River and trillions of stars watched as I followed what felt like a bridge across an abyss. My hands and face collided against absolute zero and I was nowhere.

I was meeting my girlfriend Kate the next day. I found a new energy in the anticipation. Kate and I spoke on the phone regularly; she helped me stay sane on endless stretches of road. She was bringing fresh clothes, new music, and Jorge, our Boston terrier. We were planning to spend a day and a half together outside of Memphis. I maintained a steady trot all day trying to get to her faster. The bounce of my forty-two-pound pack in full-sprint mode was certain to leave my spine two inches shorter, but it would be worth it.

The sight of her was overwhelming. My face flushed and tears came to my eyes; she had the same reaction. Jorge had a terrible head cold; his nose ran like a broken toilet and he was sneezing. But his ears went back like they always did when he saw me after getting home from work. I wanted to drive back to Chicago with them both that minute.

I jumped in the car. Kate and I melted into each other with a long hug and a kiss. We only had thirty-six hours together. Should we drive to Memphis to listen to live music? Have a nice dinner? Go to the mall for new pants? We drove to a hotel to drop off our things; once we landed on the bed, it was over.

I ended up sleeping for most of those thirty-six hours; we hardly spoke. Kate's calming influence gave me permission to relax in a way I hadn't allowed myself to since the beginning of the walk. I felt horrible for not having the energy to leave the hotel, but we were mostly just happy to be in the same room together.

Leaving Kate hurt. It was late on a gray afternoon when she dropped me off. The temperature was around forty degrees. Kate pulled over where she had picked me up, near a yellow Dollar General store. She was crying; Jorge was confused. After hugging her, I looked at her one last time and closed the car door. She drove off.

At first I had a burst of energy. I was walking so fast my staff couldn't keep up—I had to carry it. Eventually I had to stop and relax. After three hours I called Kate from a gas station. "The one with the green sign?" she said. "Yes." I said. "I drove past that ten minutes after dropping you off." There was a long silence. She was almost halfway back to Chicago.

Black forest lined both sides of the street. Finding a place to camp would be easy. I was a thousand or so miles from the Atlantic, but it felt like I was back at the ocean on the first day. I had to keep moving, but I'd never felt slower.

The next day I woke up to BB-sized sleet. The precipitation continued sporadically for a few hours and then the wind picked up around eleven. I stopped midday to build a fire and to cook macaroni and cheese. I walked with a renewed strength for four more hours after lunch and set up camp in a pine forest around five-thirty.

After my visit with Kate, I started walking at night. It wasn't so much the darkness as staring down the light of speeding cars that kept me on edge. Each time they barreled past I expected to be knocked off balance. I saw the shattered remains of armadillos littering the side of the road as I entered Memphis.

The Lorraine Motel

At sunset the next day, I stood a few feet from a concrete balcony with green railings. It was the spot at the Lorraine Hotel where Martin Luther King Jr. was killed. After his death, room 306 was removed and glass installed to view rooms 307 and 305, the last rooms in which MLK was alive. Everything rests in the position it was in on April 4, 1968: newspapers, coffee cups, and unmade beds are as he left them.

In April 1968 King was in Memphis for the second time in two weeks, supporting the Memphis sanitation workers' strike. Two thousand men, mostly African American, were demanding an increase in the seventy cents an hour the city was paying them. The wage was not enough to feed their families: nearly all the workers were on food stamps, despite working fifty hours a week. The city also refused to pay for showers, so the workers couldn't ride the bus home without the other riders being repulsed by their smell. So most workers walked home after a long day's work. The sanitation workers wore placards that read "I Am a Man!" The entire sanitation system was shut down as the men marched through downtown Memphis.

King was beginning to realize that the US economic system needed to be completely uprooted. Wealth needed to be redistributed on a mass scale if the racism was ever going away in the US. So he marched with the sanitation workers, focusing the world's attention on Memphis. The first march he led, on March 28, ended in a police riot, with hundreds of sanitation workers brutally beaten by the cops. On April 3 he returned and checked in at the Lorraine Motel.

There was a terrible storm that night in Memphis. King decided to stay back at the Lorraine and send a replacement to the Mason Temple, where he was expected to speak that night. He didn't think anyone would show up. But the Temple was filled to capacity and King's aides called him at the motel to tell him he should probably head over and address the crowd.

He ad-libbed the famous "Mountaintop" speech, which many consider his greatest and most heartfelt speech:

> And then I got into Memphis. And some began to say the threats, or talk about the threats that were out. What would happen to me from some of our sick white brothers?
>
> Well, I don't know what will happen now. We've got some difficult days ahead. But it really doesn't matter with me now, because I've been to the mountaintop. And I don't mind.
>
> Like anybody, I would like to live a long life. Longevity has its place. But I'm not concerned about that now. I just want to do God's will. And He's allowed me to go up to the mountain. And I've looked over. And I've seen the Promised Land. I may not get there with you. But I want you to know tonight, that we, as a people, will get to the Promised Land!

The next day, as King stood on the balcony outside his room at the Lorraine Motel, white supremacist James Earl Ray shot him in the face with a rifle from a distance. King was rushed to a nearby hospital, where he died. His assassination was a turning point in the civil rights struggle. The sanitation strike ended on April 16, 1968, with the workers winning increased pay and benefits. The victory was a pivotal moment for African American unions throughout the country. But the cost of winning the strike came at an extremely heavy cost—the death of the civil rights movement's greatest leader.

MEMPHIS, TN | Mile 951

Population 646,889 | Est. 1819

I met Max the next day at Donald's Donuts on Union Street, He told me his story. Four years ago he stopped in for a cup of coffee and met the owner, Quolkik, a Cambodian immigrant. Quolkik was having problems keeping her restaurant open due to language barriers and difficulties with restaurant codes. She asked Max for help. Max, who was about to turn eighty-four at the time, stepped in and built all new tables and chairs for the shop, then worked ten hours a day managing the store. Max was still maintaining the schedule. Donald's is now known for having the best donuts in Memphis. The mayor stopped in three times a week. Max had not accepted a penny in those four years; he lived on his pension. He also funded the college education of Johnny, a Donald's Donuts employee and Cambodian immigrant, who would graduate from Boston College that spring.

Max had the energy of a man half his age; he was in the Marines for thirty-one years and received the Navy Cross and two Purple Hearts for his efforts in both North Korea and Vietnam.

"Max, what about this place has kept you around so long? Ten hours a day for four years is big time investment. Is there more to the story?" I said.

"I'm more interested in how you ended up here," he replied.

I start to explain the walk, but his raised eyebrow suggested he was unsatisfied with my standard spiel. Or was I unsatisfied and he'd picked up on it?

"Max, your story is fascinating. I'd love to know more. I wish I had your energy."

"Ahh . . . you do and you don't. I'm just trying to take care of business here—to pay my dues. You know what I mean?"

As I paid my bill Quolkik's daughter Ashley said, "You don't have to pay. We want to give you something, though."

Quolkik handed me a crisp fifty-dollar bill, a bag of donuts, and three meals worth of vacuum-sealed udon noodles.

Leaving Donald's Donuts I remembered that Henry Kissinger had secretly bombed Cambodia with the code name "Breakfast, Lunch, and Dinner."

Mark Twain, Anti-Imperialist

Crossing the Mississippi River I thought of Mark Twain, who first earned a wage as a printer's apprentice in the mid-1850s. He spent four years working in East Coast cities in miserable conditions. Twain joined the printers' union and proudly boasted of his membership wherever he went. At the end of that decade he traveled back to Missouri to become an apprentice to a riverboat pilot. In

Life on the Mississippi, he describes his part in organizing a riverboat union and how it improved the lives of all riverboat workers. It was here that he learned to prefer spending time with "the mighty mass of the uncultivated" and "not with the thin top crust of humanity." Twain became convinced that strong unions were the only way forward for the United States. He read the following in union halls across the country in the 1880s and 1890s:

> When all the bricklayers, and all the machinists, and all the miners, and blacksmiths, and printers, and hod-carriers, and stevedores, and house-painters, and brakemen, and engineers, and conductors, and factory hands, and horse-car drivers, and all the shop-girls, and all the sewing-women, and all the telegraph operators; in a word all the myriads of toilers in whom is slumbering the reality of that thing which you call Power . . . when these rise, call the vast spectacle by any deluding name that will please your ear, but the fact remains a Nation has risen.

Twain and Martin Luther King would have gotten along well.

Twain also questioned his country's adventurism abroad and lived out his life as an eloquent and determined crusader against US imperialism and racism. In 1898 the United States invaded the Philippines. Twain responded, "I have read carefully the Treaty of Paris [which ended the Spanish-American War], and I have seen that we do not intend to free, but to subjugate the people of the Philippines. We have gone there to conquer, not to redeem. . . . I am opposed to having the eagle put its talons on any other land."[15]

PART II

As far as I could tell, the only road to Little Rock was Interstate 40, which would mean a long day of police questioning and possibly a ride back to Memphis. I looked at my map and saw a railroad track that ran almost parallel to it. I decided to follow the tracks until I reached Forrest City, the nearest town.

The sun set and I was surrounded by empty fields and rows of leafless trees. A bright orange-and-blue light beamed off of the rails and kept me heading in the right direction. When it was finally dark, the tracks shot out into unending emptiness. I began to feel like a ghost fruitlessly trying to make something right from a past life. I camped in a dark open field, amid a gnarled grove of trees fencing off an embankment that carried railroad tracks under a half-moon. It was a perfect spot—no electric lights, no beer cans.

I dreamed as a kid about running away and following the railroad tracks west—then my parents would be sorry. My adult version of this scenario was everything I hoped it would be: I'd be taken care of by strangers and I wouldn't need motorized transportation.

I was seventeen the last time I ran away. It happened after I punched my dad in the face, sending him to the hospital. He'd hit me first. I had been giving his live-in girlfriend Diane the silent treatment, and he said my silence sounded like a door slamming. He slammed the door twice. I didn't look up. He slammed it again. I ignored him. That's when he started hitting me in the head. I got up and slammed my fist into his mouth. He fell, I followed, and I held him down.

Diane screamed, "I'm calling the police." I stood up, soaked in his blood. I walked down the stairs—it was my blood too. I walked down the broad lawn of the house in front of ours and soon found train tracks. They looked like the stitches I would soon see on my dad's lip. It was a Tuesday. I shouldn't have been outside walking toward the city at night.

Later he asked if I'd had a roll of nickels in my hand. No, but I did have a metal statue of St. Joseph in my non-swinging hand, just in case. His question made me feel proud and disgusted at the same time. He always had a big imagination. He still has a scar.

Walking is the only way to really run away.

6

Arkansas

FORREST CITY, AR | Mile 998

Population 14,774 | Est. 1870

The next night, a warm southerly breeze kept the temperature in the mid-fifties. The only way my campsite could be accessed was by rail or a long walk. The moon peeked though clouds. I slept well when I was confident no one was around.

Around four in the morning the balmy breeze turned violent, an unmistakable sign of approaching rain. A dry tent packs pounds lighter than a wet one, so I started packing at 4:30 and was on the tracks at 4:45. When the sky broke I was soaked in seconds. I walked with my head down, guided by the white light of my headlamp and the steel and wood of the tracks, hoping a train wouldn't come. Thick cracks of lightning revealed a narrow path without guardrails across a railroad bridge, sixty feet above an angry river. I balanced for my life against the force of the gusty, cold rain. I wanted to remove my pack in case I fell; I imagined it pulling me under. I focused on the white floodlight that marked the end of the bridge. Without even remembering to use my staff, I made it across.

I walked into Forrest City later that day. The tracks ran through a historic but well-maintained downtown. One moment I was insulated by trees, the next I was avoiding traffic. I felt like a wet, hungry bear.

The rain was still heavy as I entered the post office. There were curious stares as I stood in line to send T-shirts from Memphis to Kate. Forrest City was one of the few vibrant small towns not next to a major tourist attraction that I walked through. The appliance store, the rent-to-own furniture store, and the hardware store all seemed to do good business despite the Walmart on the edge of town. I wondered what their secret was.

I met Jerry England at the Waffle House at eleven that morning. A seventy-six-year-old retired homebuilder, he made arrangements for me to meet with a reporter at the *Forrest City Times-Herald*. Jerry knew everyone in Forrest City. His wit was sharp, his energy boundless, and as I would soon find, he was not afraid to do anything.

After the interview, Jerry told me he would take me to see whatever I wanted in Forrest City. I said, "What is the town known for?"

"Nothing. Oh, actually, we have two prisons. One is state-run and it's twenty miles away; my niece works there. The other is a few miles away and it is federal."

Two prisons. So that was Forrest City's secret: it hosted one of the country's few growth industries.

I wanted to visit prisoners. Talk with them. I'd grown up Catholic, looking up to people like Sister Helen Prejean, the author of *Dead Man Walking*. I said, "Let's go to the federal jail. I'd love to talk with the prisoners."

"Sure! I don't know anyone there, but my cousin sold the government the land fifteen years ago."

"That might be our in."

The prison looked like a fallout shelter: cold, gray cinder-block walls forty feet high and miles of twenty-foot-tall fence, reinforced by rows of evil-looking coils with razor-sharp blades. There were also soccer fields, basketball courts, and a track. We parked close to the front door, in a handicapped space. Jerry has a "bionic knee," as he likes to call it. By the time we arrived at the front door, six guards were waiting for us. They were led by a tall man in his forties with a mustache, a baseball hat, and a government-issued smile.

"What are you doing here?"

I told him I wanted to talk and meet some of the prisoners. I noticed that the five other officers were standing silent with their arms crossed in a straight row, blocking the door like hellhounds.

"This is a federal penitentiary, and we don't give tours. You need to leave now, especially with that backpack."

If I had to do it all over again I would have brushed up on my Latin—the sign above the door had instructions about what to do with my hope. Walking away, all I could think of were the hundreds of men locked behind iron bars, some in solitary without a chance of human interaction for years and years.

Jerry and I went to the Saw Mill for lunch and tried to put the experience into perspective. We agreed it had been a bad idea. Billy, the owner, said his son was an Apache pilot who "fired the first shot in the first Gulf War." He comped our meals and made a generous donation. I listened to a lot of proud parents talking about their children's military adventures. Service of any sort becomes a large part of people's identity.

BISCOE, AR | Mile 1,038

Population 476 | Est. 1810

When I walked through the eastern outskirts of Biscoe, Arkansas, I saw playpens with three of four sides missing, washing machines that appeared to have withstood dynamite blasts, a zoo's worth of cracked and broken lawn animals, and decomposing cars, trucks, school buses, and tractors. They lined two miles of Highway 70. Amid all the trash I saw a sign that read "Flea Market." All of the garbage was for sale.

I had a lengthy talk with Tomeka at the Quick Stop gas station. She recently graduated nursing school while working two jobs, the other at a clothing store. She was raising three kids by herself and they all received straight As. The kids helped clean up around the house so she would have more time to study for her nursing boards. Tomeka hoped to get a job at the VA hospital after she passed the nursing tests. Most VAs are underfunded and understaffed, so Tomeka's work ethic would be put to good use.

"Man, I wish I could be walking with you. It would be good to get away, have time to reflect. I love my kids. I don't love my jobs but I know I'll love being a nurse. Sometimes I feel like I have no time to think. I mean it gets quiet sometimes behind the register here but it's still work . . . Damn, I wish I had more time to think. I bet you can think about a lot of things out there," Tomeka said.

"Yeah. That's one of the good things about this. I can think a lot. You should come walk with me for a day. I could use the company. I promise I won't talk too much."

"I'd love to, but I'd probably get fired. You take work when you can get it around here. I have too much responsibility to do what you're doing."

I wanted to talk to her for much longer but clouds were rolling in and I had to find a place to camp.

Todd pulled over to the side of the road as I walked out of town and gave me a cup of coffee. He said he'd seen me as he was driving into Hazen and kept me in mind on his way home. He had no idea what I was doing other than walking in high winds and thought I might want to warm up with a coffee.

He'd been a Marine sniper and was present when Saddam Hussein was captured. I had started to notice how many people were connected to war in some way. Everyone seemed to have a military-related story: from Tomeka wanting to work at the VA to parents telling stories about their children's war efforts to Marine snipers pulling over to talk on the side of the street.

NORTH LITTLE ROCK, AR| Mile 1,082

Population 62,304 | Est. 1866

Cypress trees towered out of the wind-rippled bayou on the road to North Little Rock. Steam rose from the water as it was pelted by thousands of small ice stones. I huddled over a cup of coffee and biscuits, mesmerized by this primordial scene on the side of the road. Hunter Riley from the Foundation, who was a Little Rock native, had told his Aunt Carolyn that I was less than a few miles from her home, so she had dropped off the food and coffee. I expected a crocodile to peek above water and make a lunge for one of Carolyn's biscuits. Maybe beauty can't be ranked. If you look close enough at anything lovely, all else ceases to exist.

Marylin Riley, Carolyn's twin sister and Hunter's mom, invited me over for dinner with her family. John, her husband, gave me a brief tour of the neighborhood before dinner—including the house from the opening scene of *Gone with the Wind*. The next day they showed me Little Rock High School, famous as a historic scene of desegregation.

The Little Rock Nine

A few hundred years late, in 1954, the US Supreme Court ruled in *Brown v. Board of Education* that segregation was illegal. However, Southern states ignored the ruling and continued to ban integration. It was not until 1957, when Minnijean Brown, Thelma Mothershed, Ernest Green, Jefferson Thomas, Terrence Roberts, Carlotta LaNier, Elizabeth Eckford, Gloria Ray Kalmark, and Melba Pattillo Beals, also known as the "Little Rock Nine," took it upon themselves to integrate the Little Rock school district that things began to change. After making their plans, they postponed their action for one day. Unfortunately, Elizabeth Eckford did not hear about the postponement and faced the angry crowd alone. Composed and steady, she approached the school wearing sunglasses and holding her books tight, but the National Guard turned her away.

The following day the Little Rock Nine entered school amid a ferocious wave of abuse from a mob of racist Little Rock residents who spat and swore at them. This act of courage would inspire civil rights activists across the South to pursue similar measures in other cities. All nine received the Congressional Medal of Honor in 1999.

HOT SPRINGS, AR | Mile 1,135

Population 35,193 | Est. 1832

I wore my gloves all day for the first time. The temperature spent the day in the low thirties and the sun struggled in a thick web of clouds. My shoulders, back, legs, and feet were dutiful friends. Occasionally during the day I would take time to celebrate the orchestra of parts and motion involved in a step. Blood, tendons, skin, nerves, and bone reach, carry, flex, and sometimes strain—step after step, mile after mile.

Before I turned off into the woods to camp, a white Cadillac Escalade slowed down. A woman peeked out the passenger side window. "Are you the guy walking across the country?"

I said yes, and she and the driver gave me the thumbs up and drove off. I saw a beautiful grove of pine trees across the street and crossed to set up my tent. A sign that read "Hunting Camp, No Trespassing" hung from a nearby tree. I wanted to ignore it, but something told me to leave—there would be a less threatening space down the road. As I stepped back onto the road, the same white Escalade pulled up and Kristen and her husband asked me if

I wanted a home-cooked meal and a warm bed. With a forecasted temperature of seventeen degrees that evening, I said yes right away. I met Kristen's husband Matt, their four-year-old son Steele, and the baby, Mattie Grace. I felt particularly dirty sitting on the black leather seats of the new Cadillac and hoped I didn't smell.

Matt and Kristen Everhart seemed to live storybook lives in Hot Springs. You could see the lake from every room of their house, which was newly remolded in a French farmhouse design. The family was in the tire business. "Everyone needs tires, even in a bad economy," said Matt. His parents Kim and Monte came over and we drank whiskey and swapped stories until midnight.

The next morning, Matt dropped me off where he had picked me up. I noticed multiple billboards with Monte's jovial face advertising tires as I walked into town. Monte arranged a meeting with the local paper and three radio shows. Monte and Matt knew almost everyone in Hot Springs. We couldn't walk ten feet without someone saying hi. And, thanks to Monte, if you were listening to a radio in Hot Springs you'd probably heard all about the walk and the Pat Tillman Foundation. I spent almost an hour total talking on four different stations. They invited me to stay longer, since it was Christmas Eve, but I didn't want to impose.

The Everharts called their close friend Brian, who arranged a motel and a Christmas Eve dinner in Crystal Springs for me. I walked into my room to find gifts waiting for me: brownies and beef jerky from Brian. I relaxed, eating beef jerky and watching *It's a Wonderful Life* on a fuzzy black-and-white TV, and thought about the incredible outpouring of support the last few days. Hot Springs was a Bedford Falls for me—at least as much of Bedford

Falls as I was ever going to see. Despite sitting alone in the motel on Christmas Eve, the images of everyone I'd met those last two days and the previous few months filled the room. Feeling appreciated and relevant, I fell asleep with the movie on.

MOUNT IDA, AR | Mile 1,171

Population 1,076 | Est. 1890

I met Larry in Mount Ida, the "Crystal Capital of the World," at Atlantis Found, one of the town's dozen crystal shops. He was skinny, with wild salt-and-pepper hair. He said the name of the store was inspired by subtle but discernible triangles found on "recorder crystals." Ancient lore, he explained, says the lost civilization of Atlantis encoded a complete philosophical and cultural library using the triangles on these crystals. He went on to describe how and why the crystals were formed: "During the continental collision that formed the Ouachitas [a local mountain range] sixty-five million years ago, hot fluids rich in silica were forced up through fractures in the uplifted stone and precipitated quartz crystals into veins within the rock. In the sandstone of the Crystal Mountains near Mount Ida lie some of the world's richest deposits of the crystals."

He described a woman who had sold him some very unusual crystals. "They looked identical in shape, texture, and color to the crystal made by the Himalayan Mountains. No one else made the connection." He continued, "I paid the woman an undisclosed but handsome figure for each piece." Larry has yet to find an acceptable explanation for the anomalous gemstones, but he believes they carry a powerful and enigmatic force. He gives them to people he feels are called to them. Larry told me his gift is his ability to place crystals with the right people. He gave me one of his "most complex" pieces to carry in a handmade leather satchel. He said it would amplify my psychic ability.

Larry believed strongly in what he was saying, and it was contagious; I wanted to believe him. He stirred my imagination. He gave life to what looked like ordinary pieces of rock.

Some say this type of thinking is silly or even dangerous, because it can be a form of denial and escapism—like all religion. But even if what Larry was saying was made up, he was able to tell a story about himself and his longings through his belief in the crystals.

NORMAN, AR | Mile 1,179

Population 423 | Est. 1910

Drew's grandfather Lee drove him two hours to Melba's Café. They waited more than an hour for me to arrive. Drew was seven years old and had been following my walk for quite some time when he decided to call the phone number that I posted on my website to ask if I would meet him and his grandpa. When I finally walked in, Drew came up to me and said, "Pat Tillman was a great man because he gave up 3.6 million dollars and a job with the Arizona Cardinals to serve his country. He was killed by friendly fire . . . I like that you are walking for his memory."

We talked a little while and then Drew handed me a red piece of construction paper to sign. Then he handed me a hundred-dollar check for the Pat Tillman Foundation. He stood as tall as my shoulder as I sat. Drew's grandfather stood over us both. I thanked them both and we said our goodbyes.

Back on the road, though, I couldn't help thinking about the military Pat had served—the military that had lied about his death, the military whose fingerprints seemed to be everywhere I turned.

They sent me to Afghanistan for the second time twelve hours after I formally declared my intentions to file conscientious objector paperwork. I shouldn't have been sent. CO status is a big deal in the Ranger Battalion—and they wanted none of it. So instead of letting me fill out the necessary paperwork, they sent me to "walk with the donkeys" in a supply role in a combat zone. I would also be the gofer for my first sergeant, who was now referring to me as "bitch" and "vile piece of shit" for betraying the Ranger Creed. If you're not familiar with it, this is the Creed:

> **R**ecognizing that I volunteered as a Ranger, fully knowing the hazards of my chosen profession, I will always endeavor to uphold the prestige, honor, and high esprit de corps of my Ranger Regiment.
>
> **A**cknowledging the fact that a Ranger is a more elite soldier who arrives at the cutting edge of battle by land, sea, or air, I accept the fact that as a Ranger my country expects me to move further, faster and fight harder than any other soldier.
>
> **N**ever shall I fail my comrades. I will always keep myself mentally alert, physically strong and morally straight and I will shoulder more than my share of the task whatever it may be, one-hundred-percent and then some.
>
> **G**allantly will I show the world that I am a specially selected and well-trained soldier. My courtesy to superior officers, neatness of dress and care of equipment shall set the example for others to follow.

> Energetically will I meet the enemies of my country. I shall defeat them on the field of battle for I am better trained and will fight with all my might. Surrender is not a Ranger word. I will never leave a fallen comrade to fall into the hands of the enemy and under no circumstances will I ever embarrass my country.
>
> Readily will I display the intestinal fortitude required to fight on to the Ranger objective and complete the mission though I be the lone survivor.
>
> Rangers lead the way![16]

I'm sure I both betrayed and honored almost every word in this code. I wasn't ready to go AWOL, so I couldn't protest the orders to Afghanistan. I was trying to stand up for what I believed in and I didn't think running away would prove that.

For the second time, I embarked on a twenty-one-hour plane ride followed by a two-hour helicopter trip. Despite the noise of the machines that transported us and the loud conversations of the soldiers all around me, all I remember was silence. I can't recall anyone saying a word to me during that trip. No one had any time for a conscientious objector. I felt sorry for myself—and scared. I pretended like I was a duffel bag and buried myself in an empty nook in the large C-5 plane we traveled in. We were dropped off somewhere in southwest Afghanistan to occupy a grade school. Classes were cancelled to make room for our new headquarters.

I had no idea what we were doing there and I don't think the chain of command did either. Lacking a clear-cut objective, they invented one by tramping about in the high mountain terrain, bored and scary, trying to gather information about the network that was potentially supporting the Taliban.

Occasionally our camp would be fired on. We lost one man to an IED—Sergeant Blessing. The shock of the initial news sent the blood rushing out of my face, arms, and legs and into my stomach. A faint buzzing sound filled my ears. I overheard the news as it came over the radio. It was nighttime and I was tired but that didn't stop my imagination from running with gory thoughts of Sergeant Blessing's final moments. Of course there wasn't anyone I could talk to about it; I was a pariah. I missed Pat and Kevin.

Young Afghan men who walked in small groups by our camp would be taken into our custody. One would be brought into one of the two dozen clay and wood-beamed classrooms we were occupying, staging from, and sleeping in to be interrogated. The rest of the group would wait in another room. Those not being interrogated would hear a gunshot. The idea was to make those not talking think that their friend had been killed and scare them into spilling some secret plan to attack the United States, or reveal the identity of someone who would. The elders in the village got wind of this quick. They'd walk down to our base and complain. No one took them seriously. Most laughed at them. I was usually off chopping wood, trying to act busy, while this was going on. I wasn't attached to a leash, but there weren't many places I could go.

When squads headed out, I had to stay at the school and continue chopping firewood. The sounds of a cheap axe splintering wood and the wind in the trees were all I would hear for hours. Occasionally I was sent off with the donkey train to gather more supplies at the bottom of the mountain. At nights I slept outside, often in the snow and the mud, by myself with a single blanket. I soon caught a high fever. There was no room for me in the rooms we were told to sleep in. The Rangers who were committed to the mission were told to set up their beds first. If there was room left over, I could squeeze in. There never was. "Sorry, Fanning. Maybe tomorrow," someone would always say with a smirk. I stopped trying after a while. In the beginning I was overwhelmed. I tried to force myself to cry to relieve the pressure, but nothing would come out. I prayed my fever would turn into pneumonia. I ate little. I didn't know how long we would stay out there. I couldn't imagine getting home safely at that point. You need support when you are halfway around the world in a combat zone—this is what famously bonds soldiers together. Being rejected in such an environment has a strong effect on the nervous system.

I did everything possible to desensitize myself. I was jumpy and constantly on edge in the presence of other Rangers. The only people I felt calmed by were the Afghans on the outskirts of the school, who stared at me as I chopped wood. I chopped until I fell over with exhaustion. I'd take my shirt, jacket, and shoes off and walk around barefoot in the snow, trying to numb myself and get sicker, avoiding guard stations as everyone else slept. I wasn't ready to take a gun to my head. My belief in God at the time made me scared of suicide. I thought I would have to come back and do it all over again for failing to understand God's plan. I also couldn't bear the thought of my family, who were proud of me for "serving my country," learning that I had killed myself.

One night I was able to sneak a phone call on the satellite phone. I called my mom. It took a few seconds to connect. I imagined the phone signal bouncing off the half-moon I was watching, down to her house on the other side of the world.

"Hi Rory. How are you? It so good to hear from you." She said.

"I'm doing fine, Mom. I can't talk long. I just wanted to hear your voice. How is everyone back home?" I said.

"They are good. We all miss you."

"I miss you too."

My face tingled with embarrassment and sadness when I got off the phone. I was her oldest son, the first-born grandchild on both sides of the family. Now I was chopping wood and being called "bitch" by my first sergeant. If I made it home, I could never say a word about it. I was scared of what that would mean. My connection with my family would be damaged from the shame. I'd have to hide a part of myself because I didn't think they would ever understand what I had done.

As time wore on I fell into an isolated routine. I started to recognize the beauty of the mountains that surrounded me. They were millions of years old and had probably seen much worse than what I was going through. I started to notice the poor and innocent-looking locals change into wise and sophisticated observers. They, like me, could only watch and go about their routines as these foreign invaders ran around with heavy weapons in the pristine wilderness we were all sharing. I was now an outsider to this militarized group just as they were. I started to feel most sorry for the Rangers. They were stronger, but they looked lost.

Sometimes Rangers would run off and steal a goat to slaughter and grill, which they'd bring back and eat without me. These were once my friends. But that was over. So I just watched out of the corner of my eye. I became part of the scenery. I was there to serve and keep my mouth shut. My old squad went out on hikes to look for something they never seemed to find. Eventually, after three months, we were told we needed to go home. I was relieved, but knew I had a lot more in front of me. I had no idea I would have to stick around for another three months while they figured out how to handle my case.

GLENWOOD, AR | Mile 1,191

Population 1,751 | Est. 1909

Cindy and Sandy cared for stray dogs at their home outside of Glenwood, Arkansas, and spent much of their time maintaining their vast three-hundred-acre property. It was their answer to Central Park. Acres and acres of forest and grass were finely cut and regularly "bushwhacked." A large man-made pond housed two ducks fed a balanced diet by Sandy, in his early sixties, who reminded me of John Wayne. He had invented a machine that recycles auto paint on the assembly line and retired early.

Sandy surprised me when he wanted to talk pole shifts, rogue planets, numerology, and gold. He informed me that December 2012 would mean the end of the world. I had heard this type of thing before and felt like I had moved on from it, but I never expected to hear it come out of a man who looked like John Wayne, my dad's idol.

"I don't know if you know this, but you were supposed to meet me. We were supposed to have this conversation. I can see you understand a lot more than you let on. And you have a message that needs to be shared—you are a seer," Sandy said in his knowing voice. I heard a lot of things that didn't correspond with my understanding of the world talking with Sandy, but, like the man in the crystal shop in Mount Ida, I appreciated his attempt to have a complete worldview.

The next day the humidity was sticky and thick. My legs requested patience and my will conceded. I didn't like to admit I'd taken time off during the holidays, but I obviously did—it had taken me two weeks to walk a hundred miles. It was the first time I napped in the middle of the day. During my rest, a subtle but urgent voice sounded in the back of my head as I contemplated sleeping for ten more minutes underneath a willow tree. "No more of this nonsense," the mystery voice said. I thought of the times I used to sneak a nap after school in high school. One leg always dangled off the bed. I'd spring to my feet when I heard my dad open the door, returning from work. The sound of his shoes clomping up the stairs to the attic apartment signaled that I had about ten seconds to get into my chair and crack a book.

As I stood up, a blue pickup stopped in front of me. Jim and Carla waved. Jim said, "Hey, Rory, do you remember us from last night?" Jim, Carla, and an eight-year-old girl named Miranda were riding four-wheelers in front of Self Creek Resort—a beautiful spot next to Lake Greeson, where I took one of my favorite sunset pictures of the trip. They invited me to stay at the resort, which they maintained. I told them that Bridget and Marty in Caddo Gap were hosting me. I thanked them and we said our goodbyes. Almost twenty-four hours later on the side of the road, in the middle of nothing in particular, Jim pulled over in his pickup and handed me a $300 check gathered from the three surrounding resorts: Self

Creek Lodge and Marina, Mountain Harbor Resort, and Iron Mountain Lodge and Marina.

I walked until four, and Jim drove back out to meet me to take me back to Self Creek Resort. There I stayed in a house overlooking a river with four bedrooms, a fireplace, and a Jacuzzi on the front deck—a stark contrast to my single-person tent. The folks there cooked a giant spaghetti dinner for me that night and we toasted the walk and Pat Tillman. My face flushed with shyness from the attention, but this meant a lot to me. I needed the affirmation. We raised a total of $1,400 that night.

Bill from Self Creek, Jim, and Carla drove me back to Little Rock to meet Kathy Holt, who introduced me to Arkansas's governor, Mike Beebe.

"Come sit down," Beebe said, pointing to a shiny leather chair in front of his desk, next to a stately fireplace. As he pointed, he mouthed to his assistant, "Twenty minutes."

"This here is the Arkansas Traveler certificate, which represents the friendliness and hospitality that Arkansas extends to out-of-state visitors who have contributed to the progress, enjoyment, or well-being of the State of Arkansas to her people. The governor"—he referred to himself formally in the third person—"issues a handful of these certificates a year, with the first going to President Franklin Delano Roosevelt in 1941. A recipient pledges to spread good will for the state. Do you know the legend of the Traveler Certificate?" He handed me the certificate, which looked like a large diploma.

"I'm sorry, I don't."

"According to legend, a tired and hungry traveler came upon a humble mountain cabin and found the owner sitting in the doorway, playing a fiddle. The traveler stopped and asked the man why he only played the first part of the same old tune. The fiddler replied that he didn't know the rest of the song. Taking the fiddle, the traveler played the rest of the tune. The fiddler was so happy that he invited the traveler to share in the comforts of his home and to stay for as long as he wanted."

As he neared the end of his story, I prepared to talk about the Foundation. I couldn't help imagining all the wild things Bill Clinton had done in that office as governor.

"Since my administration took over we've brought a lot of jobs to this great state—we signed a big contract with Caterpillar just the other day."

"Really?"

"Yes, sir. You know, as a recipient of the Arkansas Traveler certificate, you promise to say only good things about this state. Are you up for the challenge?"

"Thank you, Governor, but—"

"Of course you are, you're walking across the damn country! You're up for all kinds of challenges, aren't you!"

Beebe's assistant came in and I was ushered out the door. As I left, he said, "Now don't forget your promise to say only good things about Arkansas!"

Jim dropped me off on a dirt road after my last night at Self Creek Resort. For four days, he had been picking me up after a day of walking. He'd take me back to the resort to sleep, then drive me out to where he last picked me up the morning before. It was great. He must have driven 350 miles over the course of those four days. Soon after Jim dropped me off for the last time, someone in a cowboy hat drove by in a rusty red pickup truck with jacked-up wheels and threw a Fanta can at me, yelling "hippie" as he drove off. It exploded by my leg. I thought about chasing him down, showing him my Arkansas Traveler certificate, and giving him a little talk about hospitality. But I was walking, and he was driving a jacked-up truck.

I called Kate to vent. She laughed and said, "Hurry home, or I'll be throwing more than orange pop at you the next time I see you."

Women in Norfolk, Virginia, who gave me Bible literature and two dollars on the first day of the walk.

Lorraine Hotel in Memphis, Tennessee, the site of Martin Luther King Jr.'s assassination in 1968.

Tomeka from the Quick Stop in Biscoe, Arkansas.

A sign marking the Trail of Tears National Historic Trail, authorized by Congress in 1987. The Trail covers more than 2,200 miles of land and water routes in nine states. Photo taken on the side of the road in Georgia.

Man sitting on the side of the road in Ellijay, Georgia.

Sludge and Greasy find a home near Fort Worth, Texas.

Commerce, Texas, site of
Jerald Thomas's
coffee clubhouse.

Giving my walking stick
a break in a La-Z-Boy
found on the side of the
road in Texas.

Very Large Array, fifty miles west of Socorro, New Mexico.

Six-year-old Elijah Mendez with his parents, Robert and Tracey, at Mama Tucker's Cakes and Donuts in Roswell, New Mexico.

Horses found staring at me after a nap twenty-three miles outside of Roswell, New Mexico.

Pat Tillman statue outside of University of Phoenix Stadium in Glendale, Arizona.

Cooking dinner in the Arizona desert (photo by Jennifer Kushman).

My backpack and sign (photo by Jennifer Kushman).

Salvation Mountain, California, with Haydee Rodriguez.

Official Center of the World, which is a dot on a bronze plaque within a pyramid in Felicity, California.

Dunes from the opening scene in *Return of the Jedi* near the Mexican border.

On the side of the road in Arizona (photo by Jennifer Kushman).

7

Texas

The animals were loud my first night in Oklahoma. I could hear dogs, cows, coyotes, and an owl. I wasn't in the woods because the vines at the entrance were dense, with needles sticking from them. I emerged after a brief attempt to set up camp with blood running down my arms and two holes in my tent—I would find the holes later, after the next rain. Instead I camped next to a long trailer home at the edge of a field. Guided by the light of the moon, I crept to within a few feet of the spooky trailer to make sure it was abandoned. A satellite dish that looked like a crash-landed UFO was sticking out of the roof, a hot-water heater was protruding from a closed front door, and a few broken windows assured me I would be undisturbed by corporeal visitors that night. If there were guests, they would be ghosts. I would only be in Oklahoma for thirty-three miles. Then I entered Texas, the most daunting state on my route, or so it seemed.

Jimmy Tapley, a sixty-one-year-old crop duster, picked me up in his recently acquired '87 red Corvette. He was wearing an Oklahoma Sooners hat, Wrangler jeans, a "Professional Bull Riders (PBR)" shirt and an earth-worn countenance. He was skinny as the cornstalks he talked about dusting. He said his niece Rachel had a house just across the border in Texas—I hated crossing the Texas border in a car, because I liked entering a state on foot first. I would be dropped off the next day back in Oklahoma, so I could continue to say I had walked every step from the Atlantic to the Pacific.

As we crossed the river Jimmy told me he'd once flown his plane at 213 miles an hour under the sixty-foot-tall bridge we were driving across—with his date in the co-pilot's chair. "It was killer!" he said, with wide eyes and perfectly white dentures. He said he worked from five in the morning to ten at night seven days a week, eight months a year. He was one of the top two agricultural crop dusters in the country. "I am compensated extremely well for my expertise," he said as we turned down a gravel road at almost seventy miles per hour. "In more than three decades, I have never crashed a plane." His assurances failed to loosen my grip on my seat. Jimmy talked as fast as he drove. His niece Rachel told me later that, "as a bull rider, riverboat captain, single father, helicopter pilot, and a duster, Jimmy has made and spent fortunes many times over."

Jimmy wrote a five-hundred-dollar check for the Foundation, dropped me off at the Redland store, and went to pick up a "nice young lady [he] met in the Choctaw casino parking lot a few days ago," so I could meet her. Jimmy wanted to plan a riverboat trip with me up the Mississippi River. We set a date for three years later.

Rachel took me to the Big Rock in Idabel, Oklahoma, to celebrate her friend Melissa's birthday. People from eighteen to seventy years of age come to the Big Rock to two-step and jitterbug. The women wear cowboy boots and rhinestone belts; the guys wear extra-long Wranglers and baseball hats. The Big Rock requires patrons to bring their own alcohol, which is labeled and stored under the bar for weeks. The establishment charges a service fee for each drink poured. I met nearly everyone in the packed bar.

The next day I watched Rachel manage her son Riley (six years old) and Rhett (sixteen months). She was an amazing single mother. Riley was patient and loving with his younger brother. He read above his age level and helped his mom around the house. Rhett was tireless, inquisitive, and showed early signs of a generous spirit. He gave me rugs, cowboys, remote controls, a dime, and baby food. His steady steam of offerings lasted all day. The endurance I needed to walk fifteen to twenty miles a day is nothing in comparison to raising two kids and working full time as Rachel did. It was hard saying goodbye to those boys. Rhett, who could only say a few words, reached out to hug me as I left. Riley gazed at his shoes as I walked out the door. Jimmy drove me back to where he'd picked me up in Oklahoma.

I was finally across the Texas line on my own. I felt as excited crossing the Red River as I had crossing the Mississippi. I considered myself officially in the West.

Native Americans in Oklahoma

The Cherokee, Choctaw, Chickasaw, Creek, and Seminole people were "relocated" to the Oklahoma Territory in the 1830s. It was the proverbial and literal end of the line on the Trail of Tears—or so the federal government said. It was the tribes' land "till the end of time." But the five tribes made the mistake of supporting the Confederacy during the Civil War. The Union had been breaking their treaties, slaughtering them, and moving them off the land; they thought things might be better for them if the Confederacy won the war.

After the Union won, the federal government said the Indians had forfeited their right to the land. A land rush soon followed—and so did outlaws like the James brothers and the Dalton gang, who hid out in the hills near the eastern part of the state. The Oklahoma Territory remained largely unregulated by federal law until 1893, when the Dawes Act officially dissolved the tribes, depriving them of the right to collectively occupy land. Indians now had to own the land as whites did, as individuals.

The 1890 census of the United States population determined that there were 237,000 Native Americans living north of the Rio Grande. Agricultural archeologists now estimate that in 1492, fifteen million Native Americans were living on the land now owned by the United States. This means the population had fallen by 97 percent by 1890. Native Americans were living on fifty million square acres of reservation land in 1890. This is 3 percent of the total land held by the United States at the time, a number that corresponds to the total population decrease of Native Americans by 1890.[17]

PARIS, TX | Mile 1,228

Population 21,171 | Est. 1845

Caleb, who was ten years old, was wearing a cowboy hat and a Lone Ranger T-shirt. He helped his mother run the only store between the Oklahoma line and Paris, Texas. I asked him if the store would be his one day. He said, "I guess," and shrugged. "My brother wants to be an animal doctor and my other brother wants to be a firefighter. I don't care what I do as long as it pays Mom's bills."

"You don't want to do something like your brothers?"

"Only after Mom's mortgage is paid," he said solemnly.

Mortgage comes from the Latin for "death grip." Sadly, he was right. I used to sell death grips at the bank in Chicago. It's hard to think about other things when the mortgage isn't paid.

Bruce Snyder, who was Pat Tillman's coach at Arizona State, was battling cancer and had to sit out the 2009 presentation of the Pat Tillman Award, given annually to one of the nation's top college scholar-athletes. The honoree had to exemplify Pat's leadership qualities on and off the football field. It was to be presented at the East vs. West Shrine All-Star game in Houston, Texas, the following Saturday. The Tillman Foundation asked me if I would present the award in Coach Snyder's place. I was honored by the request, but didn't know how it would affect the walk. Actually, I was more than honored. The Foundation had been hesitant to endorse the walk initially. Now they wanted me to present this wonderful award. I hadn't messed things up in the dozens of interviews I had given, and now they considered me an ambassador for the Foundation. I was overcome with joy. But I was seven miles from Paris, Texas. I had to figure out how I was going to get to Houston.

Bryan Scott, who had seen saw me walking and made a generous contribution to the Foundation the previous night, tracked me down on the side of Farm Road 195 as I was giving an interview to the *Paris News*. I told him about my need to get to Houston in a few days to present the award. He told me that he and his buddy Mike would make the two-hundred-mile round trip from Paris to the Dallas airport to ensure I caught my Thursday flight to Houston for the Shrine game.

Bryan and Mike picked me up around four-thirty on Highway 82, west of Paris. We headed towards Dallas, stopping at Dick's Sporting Goods for five days' worth of dry food. The ride was nonstop laughs. Bryan is an avid duck hunter and Mike coaches soccer in Paris. I felt like I'd won the lotto when they volunteered to pick me up the following Monday after returning from Houston to take me back to Paris—a four-hundred-mile round trip for a stranger.

HOUSTON, TX | Mile 1,228

Population 2,100,263 | Est. 1837

I was used to making a gradual entry into major metropolitan areas like Charlotte, Memphis, and Huntsville, with rural roads giving way to suburban streets and then the boulevards of a big city. Arriving so suddenly in Houston felt like stepping from a glacier onto a rocket.

The banquet, held the night before the game, honored the 200 finest college players of 2008. Sara Christenson, who was burned in a fire at a young age, spoke flawlessly in front of the 750 person crowd about what a Shriners Hospital did to help her overcome her injuries; she was president of her freshman class and a varsity swimmer. Doug Williams of the Tampa Bay Buccaneers, Brad Van Pelt of the Giants, Charley Taylor of the R**skins, and Jerry Kramer of the Green Bay Packers were inducted into the Shrine Game Hall of Fame. I sat at Jerry Kramer's table with his family and Jack Hart and his family. Gene Stallings from the University of Alabama and Bobby Ross from the San Diego Chargers handed out the awards to all the players.

The last award of the evening was the Pat Tillman Award. Jack Hart wept as he read the inscription on the plaque. Then I gave a seven-minute talk about the Pat Tillman Foundation, the walk, and the unbelievable appreciation the people I'd met on the road had shown for Pat Tillman. I handed the award to Collin Mooney, West Point's all-time single-season rushing leader with 1,339 yards. As of 2013 he was splitting his time between serving as a military recruiter and as a fullback for the Tennessee Titans. He said he had kept Pat's picture in his locker all through high school and college.

After the banquet I went upstairs for a cocktail reception. My hair was long and I was wearing a sport coat borrowed from a man much bigger and older than me. I had lost at least thirty pounds by that point. I felt like a stick figure compared to the Division I football players. But they were all very interested to hear about the walk. I wasn't really used to cocktail crowds at that point and didn't know how much permission I had to live it up, so I nursed a beer and went up to my room early.

Back on the walk, I called my dad to tell him about the weekend. "I met Jerry Kramer, and a bunch of other former NFL players. They want to support the walk. They think what I am doing is really cool!"

There was a pause, "Jerry Kramer's book on football was the first sports book I owned. I read it religiously."

"Is that so?"

"This walk sure is catching on."

"Yeah, do you really think so? Who would have thought it would turn out this way?"

". . . You tell Jerry Kramer your old man bought his book. Keep up the good work."

I said, "I will. Thanks, Dad!"

After I hung up I felt a surge of pride well with in me. I walked easy for the rest of the morning—but soon the dry wind howling through the Texas terrain left me feeling empty.

COMMERCE, TX | Mile 1,267

Population 9,250 | Est. 1872

At a quarter to five in the afternoon, with the sun a hand's width above the horizon, I saw a dozen state troopers, a few black Suburbans, an ambulance, and a helicopter escorting a limousine outside of Haltom City, Texas, on Highway 24. I didn't need a confirmation of who it was. My mind felt a billion fingers pointing at the back of George W. Bush, the world's most sensitive war criminal, now riding into the sunset, preparing for a life painting portraits of his dogs.

I entered Commerce, Texas, thinking about Bush and what the country looked like after eight years of his presidency: we were entrenched in two seemingly endless wars, the economy was devastated, and there had been no progress in the battle against climate change.

My feelings for Texas were sour as I entered Cowhill Express Coffee shop and met Jerald Thomas and his wife, Elaine. I had no idea that I was about to meet people and see a town that would inspire me for years to come. The coffee shop was filled with antiques and cowboy memorabilia. The Thomases invited me to stay in their guest cabin five miles away. As a converted cowboy-hat shop, the single-room cabin was outfitted with a century-old steel-frame bed and an equally old cowboy quilt. The cabin had a wood floor painted red, a signed picture of Jerry Biggs from *Lonesome Dove*, who lived down the road, wooden chairs surrounding a small wooden table, kerosene lamps, cowboy hats, a large leather trunk at the foot of the bed that looked like it had seen the continent on the back of a covered wagon, and numerous sepia photos of cowboys.

Jerald and his wife had also converted an old grain silo, located feet from the front door of my cabin, into a private morning-coffee clubhouse. Locals and the occasional guest speaker met at eight for coffee every morning. The regulars included Jim Ainsworth, a published author, motivational speaker, and rodeo team-roping champion; Jerry Lyle, a professor at Texas A&M Commerce; Rick Vanderpool, a professional photographer and writer and award-winning montage artist; Paul Voss,[18] owner of a big trucking firm, who had once been shot with a crossbow in Dallas; Michael Johnson, a motivational speaker and author of children's books; Dennis Wilson, who heads the Commerce, Texas, department of housing; and of course Jerald, the host, who had been the first person to successfully sell frozen cappuccino in Texas. He appeared regularly on QVC, offering a hundred kinds of flavored coffee. Jerald had recently finished a 326-mile horseback ride with his buddies and owned a large portion of downtown Commerce.

Jerald knocked on my cabin door at seven-thirty the following morning with a fresh-brewed cappuccino and homemade biscuits. We headed for the grain silo, where he built a fire and the guys slowly filtered in. A potbelly stove stood on a red brick floor in the center and various cowboy artifacts hung on the inside, along with a painting of a brunette with one nipple exposed. I asked Jerald if they had any women in their coffee club. Kindly, he said, "We don't turn anyone away." I left it there.

Michael Johnson, in his early sixties, spoke first. Michael had steel-blue eyes, pressed Wranglers, polished tan boots, and a black cowboy hat and wore a kerchief around his neck which rested just below a face resembling William H. Macy. He talked about a traveler he had come across who was circling the eastern half of the United States in a rowboat. The thirty-one-year-old traveler told Michael a story of another man he'd met, on the banks of the Mississippi. The man had told him, 'Your arms will explode in a few weeks if you continue along using those wooden oars.' Then he ran up to his house and brought down a carbon-fiber oar decorated with a red letter W. The man said to the traveler, 'I won a bronze medal with these paddles. I want them back when you're done.'" The point of the traveler's story, according to Michael, was that when you set out to make the world a better place, the world rises to meet you along the way. Stories like this went on for two hours as we drank coffee and ate biscuits in the silo. I said to the group, "How did you all find each other? To be honest, I wasn't expecting this when I walked into town."

"Didn't you get the point of the last story I told?" Michael said.

I took a sip of my coffee and said, "Yes. I guess I do."

After the stories died down, I left for a day's worth of walking.

Jerald picked me up at the end of the day and brought me back to his coffee shop. Nearly fifty people gathered for a singer/songwriter night at Cowhill Express. The mayor of Commerce read a proclamation declaring January 22, 2009, Rory Fanning Day in Commerce, in honor of my efforts on behalf of the

Pat Tillman Foundation. Jerry Biggs, who played Roy Suggs in *Lonesome Dove,* signed pictures of his headshot from the miniseries for five dollars. Brad Davis, a Grammy Award–winning singer/songwriter, sold CDs. Rick Vanderpool signed posters for five dollars. All the proceeds, plus tips from the evening, went to the Foundation. We raised $357. It was all Jerald's doing. As I got under the quilted blankets that night, I felt confident, peaceful, and respected. The Commerce community, without knowing my life story, without knowing how much money I had to my name, had lifted me up. I felt unburdened, a long way from those nights I stared at the cinder-block wall on the blue mattress in Ranger Battalion.

The San Patricio Brigade

Mexico won its independence from Spain in 1821. At the time, Mexico included the territories now known as Texas, New Mexico, Utah, Arizona, Nevada, California, and parts of Colorado. With financial support from the United States, Texas broke away in 1836 and was granted US statehood on December 29, 1845. Its southern border was the Nueces River, 150 miles north of the Rio Grande (the present-day southern border of Texas). Roughly seventy-five thousand Mexican farmers occupied the area between the two rivers.

The United States looked for an opportunity to invade. The following spring, President James Polk sent General Zachary Taylor and a regiment of troops into Mexican territory, hoping to provoke a response from Mexico. Polk got his wish when Taylor's quartermaster,

Colonel Cross, was ambushed crossing the Rio Grande. His body was found eleven days later. This incident was followed by another ambush, also in held Mexican territory, where sixteen of General Taylor's troops were killed by Mexican guerillas. Taylor sent a message to Polk following these two incidents: "Hostilities may now be considered commenced."

Taylor used his troops—newly arrived immigrants who had fled Ireland during the potato famine that killed a million Irish—as bait for the invasion. Realizing this and faced with abysmal conditions,[19] Jon Riley and a few hundred Irish soldiers who felt they had more in common with the Catholic Mexican troops they were supposed to be fighting mutinied against their US officers. Kerby Miller, the renowned historian of the Irish emigration to America, writes that the Irish soldiers "realized that the [US] army was not fighting a war of liberty, but one of conquest." They saw Mexico, like Ireland, as a nation being "taken over and exploited by a much richer and powerful neighbor."[20] The song "St. Patrick's Battalion" was written to commemorate this mutiny:

> We were the red-headed fighters for freedom
> Amidst these brown-skinned women and men
> Side by side we fought against tyranny
> And I daresay we'd do it again
> . . .
> From Dublin City to San Diego
> We witnessed freedom denied
> So we formed the Saint Patrick Battalion
> And we fought on the Mexican side.

The San Patricios fought bravely, but eventually ran out of ammunition and were besieged and captured. The US Army tortured them and sentenced forty-eight to death by hanging. They cheered the Mexican flag from the gallows. An eyewitness described them: "Hands tied, feet tied, their voices still free." At 9:30 a.m., as the U.S. flag appeared, the horses were whipped, and the men died.[21]

On February 2, 1848, the Treaty of Guadalupe Hidalgo was signed to end the war. As a result, the United States acquired more than half a million square miles of land, now fiercely guarded from "illegal" Mexican "immigrants." The men of the St. Patrick's Battalion are still honored throughout Mexico every March 17.

ROYSE CITY, TX | Mile 1,299

Population 9,349 | Est. 1885

I ordered a turkey sandwich and a coffee at the Well Coffee Lounge and called John Wooten, president of the Dallas chapter of the NFL Alumni Association, to talk about bringing more attention to the Foundation and the walk. John and I discussed a game plan to rally NFL alumni and current players in support of the walk. He invited me to attend a meeting that Monday. It was quite a thrill to be collaborating with NFL greats. These men revered Tillman. They knew what his sacrifice meant and they wanted to help, like so many other people had across the country. I'd soon learn that these larger-than-life NFL greats felt just as vulnerable as anyone else when they considered their futures. Many NFL alumni don't have health insurance, despite having built a billion-dollar industry. Head injuries from playing for years without proper protective equipment have reduced the average lifespan of an NFL retiree to fifty-five years, twenty less than the average white male.[22] The NFL, up until that point, had taken no responsibility and had refused to pay for adequate health care to treat conditions resulting from these players' on-the-job injuries. These men were exploited—and they wanted to bring attention to their cause. They saw Pat's life and his sacrifice of a $3.6 million contract as an appeal to the better nature of the owners and bosses—just as I had.

Inspired by my conversation with Wooten, I decided to press on well past dark. I couldn't wait to get into Dallas. The miles were easy. I felt strong. I was almost keeping pace with John Coltrane's *Giant Steps*. I didn't know if I was walking fast to meet those players or to call my dad again to tell him the details. I knew he would be proud. It seemed like the level of support for the walk increased with every town I walked through. I'd had no idea what I was getting into when I started walking. I didn't know anyone I could reach out to then, but now people were reaching out to me. The world did feel like it was rising to meet me, just as Michael had said. I pushed on, lost in my thoughts, until nine that night.

DALLAS, TX | Mile 1,333

Population 1,197,816 | Est. 1841

I entered Dallas at midday and did a radio interview, then went to the Scottish Rite Hospital to meet with the NFL Alumni Association. I met Mike Curtis, Lee Roy Jordan, Robert Newhouse, Tom Rafferty, Mike Conley, Preston Pearson, Bill Krisher, Hurles Scales, Ken Jolly, Bob Kilcullen, Jim Ray Smith, and others. They all dwarfed me, even in retirement. I was reminded again how thin I was getting. Mike Curtis, a four-time Pro Bowler who played fourteen seasons for three different teams and is widely considered one of the toughest and meanest players in NFL history, brought the meeting to order. The room wasted no time in getting to the main issue: their desperate need for medical benefits for their broken bodies. They told horror stories of their friends who were dying alone in their living rooms because they couldn't afford health insurance. They talked about dementia and Alzheimer's setting in on NFL players as early as their late forties. I had no idea things were so bad for retired NFL players. The owners had kicked them to the curb and so did the people who thought health care wasn't a universal right in the richest country in the world. It was heartbreaking.

At the end of the meeting, I gave a five-minute pitch for the walk. They hung on my every word; I forgot about how small I was compared to them and soon felt like a giant. They saw hope in the walk. They seemed inspired by it. They all voted to endorse it. Preston Pearson, who was a rusher, receiver, and kick returner in five different Super Bowls, said, "We will do our best to promote your cause if you can help us promote ours." Of course I agreed. Preston was good friends with Michael Irving, who had a popular radio show in Dallas. Preston would try to book me on the show. Under the name of the Retired Professional Football Players of Dallas, they voted to donate a thousand dollars to the Pat Tillman Foundation. I was ecstatic, deeply moved, and motivated to collaborate in any way I could.

The minute-keeper for the meeting was Jen Walter, a linebacker for the Dallas Diamonds, a women's pro football team. She would go on to be the first woman to play on a professional men's football team. She said she would help promote the walk among the Diamonds. Jen had pursued her passion and dreams in spite of sexism. She loved football and the Independent Women's Football League (IWFL). She was working on her doctorate in sports psychology and had taken an active lead in promoting the league. At five foot two, she had to spend twice as much time in the gym as the other women playing the same position. Her arms looked like those photos of floating glaciers, with equal parts of rock and hard ice above and below the water. She walked with me for a few hours outside of Dallas.

After a brief stop at the famous grassy knoll where President Kennedy was assassinated, Leslie, my talkative and kind waitress at the Cliff Restaurant, donated five dollars to the walk and told me to make sure I stopped by the grave of Clyde C. Barrow—as in Bonnie and Clyde. He rests next to his brother Marvin "Buck" Barrow in Western Heights, a small and neglected cemetery on a busy street. Clyde's grave is less than twenty feet from an auto-repair garage. Loud Mexican music played and graffiti was spray-painted on the garage's aluminum siding. Offerings of bread crusts and heroin bags in short pottery cups with black Chinese symbols rested on his flat headstone. It seemed odd that such infamous and celebrated outlaws were crammed into such an unglamorous resting place. I tipped my hat and headed out.

I could not find a place to camp that night. I walked until nine, passing dozens of thirty-dollar-a-night motor lodges, with names like The Oasis, Paradise, and The Ritz. The only other business that surpassed them in number was bail-bond stores. I could have probably squeezed behind a building or two, but the bright marquees over said establishments would have guaranteed uneasy rest. Finally, as I neared Fort Worth, I found a few large cedar bushes in between a mansion and some railroad tracks. The sprinkler system for the mansion kicked on and sprayed my tent all night.

I called my dad, excited to tell him about recent developments.

"Hey there, bud. How are you? I just shot a twelve-point elk!" he said.

"That's great!"

"Yeah, the rack is huge."

"Very cool! . . . I finally had a chance to sit down with the NFL greats!" I ran down a list of names.

"Sure, I remember watching those guys play. Mike Curtis was absolutely one of the toughest in the game. They called him 'the Animal,' haha! I remember the time when a fan ran out onto the field during a Colts game trying to steal the football. Everyone stood by and watched Curtis run up and level the guy. Wham—he really laid him out!"

"I bet he did!" I laughed with him. "You know, I learned some interesting things from these guys. The NFL owners have totally abandoned them."

"Yeah, they certainly didn't make the money players are making now. It's too bad."

"Yeah, but these guys are in bad shape—players that built the NFL and turned it into a billion-dollar business. These guys have a life expectancy of barely fifty. How much money is twenty years of life worth, Dad? Would you trade twenty years of life for a couple of million?"

"I don't know."

"Dad . . ." Frustrated, I struggled to find the words, then realized it wasn't worth the effort. "All right, Dad, I gotta go." I hung up feeling spent. Most of Texas was still in front of me. So were the Rockies. I limped along the rest of the day. My staff felt clunky and awkward, so I tied it across my pack with the rope Laurie had given me and walked into West Texas, chopping the heads off newly blooming spring flowers with my staff and remembering.

After ninety days in Afghanistan, we returned to the States. I expected some sort of quick decision on my case. I woke up at four-thirty every morning for the next three months to prepare the battalion kitchen for breakfast, lunch, and dinner. On a few occasions my former squad leader would call me to attention in the middle of a packed chow hall and stare at me eye to eye for a few minutes. He always looked like he was ready to explode, but never said a word. It could have been worse.

I was sent to the Second Army Ranger Battalion's chaplain. The chaplain had fought in Mogadishu and later consulted on the movie *Black Hawk Down*; everyone was in awe of him and his chiseled jaw. His job was to convince me to be okay with fighting in Afghanistan and Iraq.

"I can't kill people for the US military anymore. I thought I was doing the right thing when I entered the military. I thought I was protecting the country from terrorists. I don't feel that way anymore," I told him.

"God understands just wars. What we are doing in Afghanistan and Iraq is protecting innocent people in the US. And what about your Ranger buddies? They depend on you. God needs us to take care of the guys to the left and right of us."

"We are targeting some of the poorest people in the world. We are representatives of the richest country in the world. Is this really the best we can do? What about 'What you do to the least of my brothers you do to me'? What about the innocent people in Afghanistan—"

"Yes, yes, there is a gray area. And it is never good to kill innocent people. But we have to trust God's plan."

I stopped being able to think. He had backed me into a corner. Everything I could think to say stumbled out of my mouth; I could see he thought I was pathetic at that point. I had been talking about God's plan since high school. I didn't know how to argue back.

The only ones in the battalion who were sympathetic to my case were the Tillman brothers. They weren't scared to talk to me in public. They empathized and said, "Try not to let it get to you." Pat looked forward to getting out of the military himself, but knew his very public circumstances forced him to stick it out.

I was able to navigate the rejection I felt, my fear of explaining my situation to my parents, and the fog that was my future in large part thanks to the respect and tolerance the Tillman brothers showed me during that time.

HALTOM CITY, TX | Mile 1,354

Population 43,376 | Est. 1932

Jim Ainsworth from Commerce, Texas, one of the great men I sat and talked with over coffee in Jerald Thomas's grain silo, had told me, "If you walk through Fort Worth, be sure to stop by and say hi to Annie Golightly. You won't regret it."

He gave me her phone number. I took Jim at his word and walked to Haltom City, a suburb eight miles north of the heart of downtown Fort Worth. When I knocked on her door, Annie greeted me with a firm handshake. Her long, eighty-year-old fingers wrapped around my hand with ease. Her salt-and-pepper hair was pulled back in a ponytail. She seemed annoyed by my rough-looking appearance.

She offered me coffee and we sat down.

"I was a mother, grandmother, and great-grandmother. I buried two husbands, raised five kids alone, survived a flood that destroyed my home—Arnold Palmer helped raise the money to build me a new one—lost my nightclub, and then lost everything that was left in a fire. At sixty-two and in financial ruin I decided to go to college for a degree in English. In 1995, when I was sixty-five, thirty working cowboys and I left Fort Worth to move three hundred longhorns 1,500 miles to Miles City, Montana. We were retracing the steps of the cattle drive in Larry McMurtry's *Lonesome Dove*. I was initially told there would be no working women on the drive. I could only go as an entertainer for the rodeos that would be organized along the route. I was allowed on the trip because I played guitar and sang country western and jazz for a good portion of my adult life, and was relatively well known in Fort Worth and Dallas. During the six-month cattle drive I slept on the rough earth in a bedroll, endured freezing rain and snow."

Annie, in the words of Jim Ainsworth, "not only drove the cattle but ended up running the show."

Annie smiled at me. "You have a dream like I had, Rory. I hope you continue to follow it. Whatever your fears and demons are, they can be purged if you set your eyes on something bigger than you. Committing to your goals and never quitting will help you to become more creative. And it is creativity that brings us happiness. I know you will find what you are looking for someday."

She was packing up her house with her son and daughter-in-law that day. They were moving her to a retirement home to recover from her two recent strokes.

It was time for a beard trim. I walked into Herbun Health Foods looking like a hippie, so I was expecting a warm reception. Well-being, healing, relaxation, and health were heavily advertised outside. No cell phones were allowed because of the live bees kept in the backyard. A woman stopped me at the front door and said, "Whoa, whoa, hold on! Whatever you need, I will bring it to you! There's a lot of art in here and I don't want you breaking it with that pack." I didn't feel like taking off the pack. Tired and annoyed by her tone, I turned around and left, mumbling something about false advertising. It has been my experience that often we sell and teach what we need to own and learn the most. Down the road, the manager of Grandy's Restaurant pointed his finger at me and then at the door three steps into his restaurant—meaning he wanted me to leave. "Sorry, we can't accommodate your large pack in here," he said. I scowled at him and left.

OUTSIDE OF FORT WORTH, TX
Mile 1,361

Population 741,206 | Est. 1849

I climbed a rusty barbed-wire fence with the help of my staff and set my tent up next to a cactus nest. Dry brush and dormant Texas witch-hair trees kept me hidden from a two-story brick house with an automatic sprinkler system that sounded like a rattlesnake den. I managed to stay away from the spray that night. The temperature dropped twenty degrees less than an hour after the sun pulled the covers over its head for the night.

The next day, as I sat on the side of the road eating a Pop-Tart, two dogs jumped in my lap. I fed them half the Pop-Tart, assuming they had run over from the nearby ranch. After a few minutes of watching them mock-fight over my attention, I picked up and started walking. They walked with me for two hours. The black dog (I named him Sludge) never got more than twenty feet in front of me without stopping to wait. He passed the time playing catch with a plastic bottle he carried in his mouth. I named the white dog Greasy; he followed six inches behind my heels. Sludge had a rabies-vaccine tag on his collar but no other ID. Greasy was without a collar. I walked by a rundown house with a dozen cars on the front lawn and four children jumping on an orange plastic bench seat that had once belonged to a van. Sludge ran up to the kids and they started hugging him. I continued walking; Greasy kept at my heel. After a few minutes, I turned around and headed up the sandy driveway to see if I could secure a quick adoption. I saw three men, all wearing either overalls or camouflage, working on a cart designed for a horse. I introduced myself and said the dogs were well behaved, most likely going to get hit by a car, and needed each other; would they mind keeping them? Two of the men ignored me but one man with overalls, a red NASCAR hat, and a large medicine-ball stomach said, "Yeah, that highway sure will get 'em. I think I'll keep 'em for the kids." I thanked everyone, took a picture of the family, and headed back to the road.

MINERAL WELLS, TX | Mile 1,409

Population 16,788 | Est. 1881

Laura, also known as "Spud," at the Jitter Beans Roasting Company shared with me a brief history of Mineral Wells and the famous, abandoned Baker Hotel, which sat across the street from us. The early Hollywood elite thought they'd found the fountain of youth in Mineral Wells. The town's cure-all water made everyone who drank it feel invincible. Judy Garland, Clark Gable, and the Three Stooges all came to the Baker to drink the water. The FDA, however, stepped in during the forties and said the town needed to explain what made the water so good. After a few tests, it was discovered that the secret was in fact lithium. The jig was up. The water was soon purified and the town lost some of its mystique.

David Adams, whom I met in front of the Mineral Wells Lions Club, introduced me to his friends Jimmy and Jane Baldwin, who invited me to stay at their Art Ranch. It overlooked the Brazos River on an elevated plateau. We were greeted by a large cedar-and-iron gate that opened to a two-story stucco and Spanish-tile hacienda. I felt like I was on a Sergio Leone movie set. We walked to their great room, where two large stone fireplaces bracketed a hundred-foot hall with wagon-wheel light fixtures and classic Western barn doors that opened onto a magnificent courtyard. Thirty guest rooms, a yoga studio, and an art gallery circled the courtyard. Enormous glass windows offered an endless vista. I walked the long room and saw dozens of abstract paintings, photographs, effigies, and shaman masks. The ranch had been preserved to maintain the integrity of the midcentury Spanish/Western architecture and interior design, but also to express the creative energy of its current owners. Jimmy and Jane liken their idea to the Chautauqua movement, which began in upstate New York in the nineteenth century. Speakers, musicians, entertainers, preachers, and artists still gather there to improve the local population's mind and body. Jimmy, a singer-songwriter whose album *Somebody's Nobody* made it to the Top 40 Americana chart in 2008, was the creative director for a major advertising firm in Dallas. Jane is a yoga therapist, poet, columnist for two children's magazines, and anthropologist who studied the Maya in Belize. We chatted late into the night.

The next day, David and his son Jett (named after the NFL football team) picked me up at the end of a gorgeous sixteen-mile walk through the Brazos River valley. We drove to their house in Mineral Wells, where his wife Alison, daughter Chloe, and son Miles were waiting for us with carne asada and a pitcher of fresh margaritas. I was surrounded by creature comforts again. I woke to fresh homemade cappuccino and breakfast burritos. Jett, who was in first grade, went into his pirate-chest bank and took out twenty dollars for the Foundation. I gave him my YoYo-Jam Super SpinFaKtor yo-yo in return—I had been yo-yoing to pass the time since Virginia. Before I left, David gave me his iPod to walk with, loaded with five thousand songs. It was exceptionally generous. I tried to protest over such an expensive and perfect gift, but my act was short-lived. I walked that day straddling feelings of profound gratefulness and suspicion of my happiness—I wanted to keep walking forever, but knew I couldn't.

Steve and Steve picked me up for dinner the next night. They had driven ninety miles from Brownwood, Texas, to talk. They organized the Brownwood Human Rights Committee, where they drew attention to injustice in and outside the LGBTQ community in Texas. They also owned Steves' Market and Deli, where they proudly displayed a Pat Tillman jersey on the wall. They were both deeply moved by Pat's life. We sat down and chatted for two hours over dinner and talked about the challenges living as an out member of the LGBTQ community. They had been Tillman Foundation donors for quite some time and had heard about the walk through the newsletter. They offered to help spread the word about the walk.

The Great Peace March for Global Nuclear Disarmament

In Mineral Wells I met Wynelle, who in the 1980s walked across the country with a thousand other people to help stop the nuclear arms race. It was called the Great Peace March for Global Nuclear Disarmament. Wynelle said, "Our group conducted educational workshops along the way in schools and community centers. We ended up speaking with a million people during the nine months that we walked 3,700 miles from Los Angeles to DC. I firmly believe the march was responsible for the Reagan/Gorbachev treaty, which destroyed medium- to short-range nuclear missiles. It was signed six months after we made it to DC."

The logistics behind a thousand-person cross-country peace march were complex: from tents to toilets to washing machines, they were a moving town with its own elected officials. If a thousand people could walk across the country to fight nuclear weapons, I wondered, what would ten thousand or a hundred thousand accomplish in the fight against greed and exploitation? The secret is numbers. Wynelle understood that.

BRECKENRIDGE, TX | Mile 1,459

Population 5,780 | Est. 1876

I met Shai Berry at L&L Diner in Breckinridge, Texas. We began to talk and she soon told me about her work.

"Mike, a close family friend of mine, was recently shot at by the police fifteen times in his truck after he rolled into a fence drunk. The police claimed Mike went for his hunting rifle [which was later proven to be unloaded] when asked to exit the vehicle. After a twenty-four-hour investigation and no witnesses, Mike's truck, with fourteen bullet holes in it—the fifteenth shot blew his head off—was given back to the family. It was determined the shooting officers followed protocol and were exonerated of any wrongdoing." Shai continued angrily, "Mike's uncle Jim and I sensed a cover-up. At risk to my husband's job at the local penitentiary, we started a Justice for Mike campaign." Support was initially strong; many in the nine-thousand-person community rallied behind the cause. However, their numbers eventually dwindled out of fear and diminished interest.

She shook her head. "Uncle Jim was fired after thirty years of flawless employment at the local gas station for spearheading the campaign. The company had close ties to the city and they were pressured to fire him. I was beginning to lose hope. I felt like the institution I was up against was too powerful. Then I heard about the walk for Pat Tillman coming through Breckenridge. I saw it as a sign from Mike to continue the fight."

The police are now under a gag order, and no one is talking while a third investigation, demanded by Justice For Mike, winds down. Shai swore she wouldn't rest until the truth was revealed. A few years later, as I was writing this book, Shai updated me on the case: Mike's family had finally been awarded a small settlement. And because the Justice for Mike campaign raised awareness of corruption, several people have come forward to report other incidents of police brutality.

I started to look for camp about ten that night. As I walked through Breckenridge, a man pulled over in a white pickup and said, "At first I thought you were a demon walking down the side of the road. Then the more I thought about your cane and the side of the road you were walking on"—against what little traffic there was—"I thought you might be Jesus. I was recently saved after a rough divorce and figured I should see what your story was." There haven't been many Monday nights in my life where I have been mistaken for both the devil and Jesus.

After I left the military, the hardest thing I had to do was look someone in the eyes. I was afraid I would be exposed for breaking my oath. I could rationalize all of the reasons I left. The military breaks its oath to soldiers all the time: its "stop-loss" policy allows it to extend soldiers' contracts indefinitely in times of war, which is convenient during times of endless war. The US government spends 760 billon dollars a year on "defense," more than the next ten countries in the world combined. I knew US imperialism was destroying the planet, but still felt guilty for leaving. Where did the guilt come from? I thought about this type of thing often, particularly in West Texas where there was nothing to distract me.

I saw a baby wild hog with a black-and-white coat, stuck and grunting under a barbed-wire fence. I pried the fence off him with my staff, and he walked under a nearby branch and became stuck again. I moved the branch. He stopped and looked at me, grunting, like he was trying to catch his breath. He seemed lost and depressed. I had a hard time even looking at this little hog. I walked a little further and noticed his mother lying dead, hit by a car.

ANSON, TX | Mile 1,510

Population 2,430 | Est. 1882

I met Laurie, a reporter for the *Western Observer* (est. 1833), at a diner in Anson. She was wearing an American-flag shirt with an American-flag brooch. Anson is named after the last president of the Republic of Texas, Anson Jones. Laurie and her editor Tiffany thoughtfully arranged for me to stay in the Morning Star Inn that night, then took me to Dairy Queen to show me how delicious a shot of vanilla syrup in Sprite can be. We then went to the town museum where I met Bill Carman, the seventy-six-year-old volunteer curator. He had spent twenty years in the Air Force, then was hired by the Foreign Service to look for bugs and wiretaps at US embassies in Russia and Africa. The majority of the bugs, he confided, were not Russian or foreign but American. The CIA was more interested in spying on US citizens inside the embassies than the Russians were.

ROBY, TX | Mile 1,540

Population 643 | Est. 1915

I received a call from Principal Heath of Roby High confirming my arrival. I told him I was three miles out and would eat breakfast before I came over. "Don't eat too much," he replied. "We have breakfast here at the school for you."

I crossed the city limit and saw dense webs of cotton interwoven with the sturdy Texas prairie grass. Roby is a one-red-light town.

I was greeted with a box of delicious donuts. The student body amounted to no more than a hundred kids. I spoke and answered questions for forty minutes, and they listened with respect and interest. Their questions were thoughtful and sometimes funny. One boy asked me, "Do you collect antiques as you walk?" "Do you mean artifacts?" I asked, still a bit confused. He said, "No, antiques . . . I mean, souvenirs!" The crowd giggled and I said, "Yes, I just found a 180-year-old dresser in Fort Worth. It's strapped to my bag."

Another boy asked, "Which branch of the military is the best? I'm probably going to join after I graduate." His comment was met with nods of approval from many of the teachers and students.

"I don't think you should join any of them." I said. The air went out of the room.

I couldn't believe I'd just said that. My face turned red despite my best efforts to appear confident. In an empty voice I continued, "I mean, you should do what you love, and give what you love away to the world. I don't think anyone could really love the military." Those last words tasted like bile. I quickly called on someone else.

Afterward, Principal Heath handed me a check for $281. The high school had held a contest to see which grade could raise the most money for the Foundation; the winning class won a pizza party with me. They did this all on their own after Michelle Terry, the computer science teacher, saw me in the Abilene paper. I felt guilty accepting the donation, for reasons I couldn't wrap my head around. It was a poor town. Maybe I thought they needed to keep their money for themselves.

The next day I was officially five months into the walk. I stepped into strong headwinds over shaved red cotton fields on an empty stomach. I thought I'd packed more food than I did for the thirty-three-mile walk from Roby to Snyder. I ate a PowerBar for breakfast and a Pop-Tart for lunch. The vast plains to my right and left were lined with hundreds of tall gray wind machines, each with three long, sharp, thin blades that slowly rotate around an axis. I had to fight every visual instinct to accept the idea that these are good for the environment. If I lived in that area, I thought, I might prefer a life without electricity to the wind farms. The heavy wind seemed to cut my pace in half. My pack felt twice its size. One thing five months of walking taught me is that the long, grueling days are just that: days. They are not the whole trip. A good meal and a night's rest washes it all away.

SNYDER, TX | Mile 1,572

Population 10,653 | Est. 1882

Bob Kilcullen, Texas Tech alumnus and former Chicago Bear, had been working hard to organize a few speaking engagements at Texas Tech for me. I was scheduled to speak the following week. Since I averaged one hundred miles a week and I was only forty-eight miles from Lubbock, I had a little time to kill. I mailed Roby High's money to the Foundation and stopped at Manhattan Coffee House. The manager, Jacob, noticed me lingering. After chatting for a while, he offered me his second bedroom for the night. I agreed and set out for a few more hours of walking. Jacob said he would pick me up at the end of the day. We had Mexican for dinner with his mother Sandy, then went to the Boot Scootin' dance in Snyder. Jacob picked up his friend Katie and we danced to the Almost Patsy Cline Band playing fifties and sixties cowboy country all night. From kids to grandparents, everyone in town showed up. The hall was dimly lit with Italian lights and Texas stars—when I commented on this, someone said, "The Baptists feel more comfortable when no one can see them dancing and drinking." A few cans of beer into the evening, the band played "America the Beautiful." Everyone stood up, solemnly took off their cowboy hats, and swayed like amber waves of grain.

LEVELLAND, TX | Mile 1,686

Population 13,542 | Est. 1921

I was on the side of the road, sitting against my pack, staring blankly at a harvested cotton field, frustrated that I had only raised $150.00 for the Pat Tillman Foundation in Lubbock—in spite of being on all the major networks and in the *Lubbock Avalanche* and speaking twice—when Sheila pulled over. Sheila said, "I saw you on *Good Morning Lubbock* and I've been driving between Lubbock and Levelland"—a distance of twenty-eight miles—"looking for you. I teach at a place called Children's Hope. My partner and I were wondering if you would talk to twenty kids, eighteen of whom have been severely sexually abused and taken away from their parents. They're all really good young kids, but can lash out against anyone. They often cut and hurt themselves and assume responsibility for what happened to them, in spite of the earliest cases of abuse occurring at the age of four. We try to keep them involved and aware of world events like Darfur and charitable causes. We think they could really benefit from hearing about your walk. Do you think you could talk to them tomorrow? The school is along your route."

"Of course I can. I would be honored," I said, flushed with humility. We arranged a time and said goodbye.

The need to get to Levelland to talk to the kids the next day kept me moving, and I ignored a few isolated campsites on the outskirts of town. I was carrying six bags of freeze-dried astronaut food that required boiling water, but the burn ban in western Texas prevented me from starting a fire—I would rather miss the occasional meal than carry the extra weight of a propane stove. The glow of fire in the dark within city limits could have gotten me arrested and fined. I found a liquor store that sold chips and grabbed two bags. Recognizing me, Sammy, the general manager, said,

"You don't have to pay for those chips." Two hours later, as I was looking for a spot to camp, Sammy and his blinding headlights pulled in front of me on the shoulder. He said, "There's a room waiting for you at the Holiday Inn two miles ahead. Thank you for what you are doing." Staggered and grateful for the kind gesture, I thanked him and made my way to the hotel.

Children's Hope program director Sonia Garza picked me up from the Holiday Inn at noon. Children's Hope is a nonprofit largely funded by the county. The kids there receive intensive psychological work, counseling, and individual care. After they turn thirteen or fourteen, they are sent to group homes or adopted. Sonia told me about a seven-year-old boy who had been in seven different homes. I went to a small cafeteria where twenty children were eating lunch. I received points, stares, and quiet questions about the contents of my pack. Adult eyes stared out of seven- to twelve-year-old faces. A wave of sadness filled me. The tone of their questions was deliberate and thoughtful. After lunch I stood up, introduced myself, and asked the children to tell me their names and ages. I then unloaded everything from my pack and passed it around: the crystal I'd received from Larry at Atlantis Found, an unused survival handbook, my GPS tracker, my compass, the astronaut food, and my walking staff. Every child had at least three questions. Theirs were no different than the ones I received from kids at other schools in the same age group. One nine-year-old girl with short brown hair raised her hand and, like a presidential debate moderator, said, "I have a comment and three separate questions. The comment is, I once saw and pet a Northern Death Adder. The first of three questions is, have you ever seen a Northern

Death Adder? The second question is, what would you do if you saw a Northern Death Adder? And finally, do you like Northern Death Adders?" I said, "What is a Northern Death Adder?" She said, "It is a snake that my grandpa caught at his house once."

The kids raised their hands and listened to each other quietly. I was surprised to see how well they listened. I expected hyperactivity to be a symptom of their abuse, for some reason. I went in the room seeing the kids through the lens of abuse, but a few questions into our time together they were just kids. The counselor's teachers and social workers seemed to do a wonderful job at Children's Hope. I can think of no more challenging or noble profession. To help these kids love freely after a life associating love with pain and wicked abuse is to be a guide through the most complicated of labyrinths. I left wanting to take all the kids with me on my walk. I wanted them to have a chance to be part of my adventure. I wanted them to see the scenery, and maybe get adopted by any one of the wonderful people I was meeting along the way.

I camped in an expansive oil field surrounded by scores of gun-drilling oil wells; they looked like confused woodpeckers. Pooled below me was surely $3.6 million worth of oil. Or so I could imagine. So close, yet so far.

WHITEFACE, TX | Mile 1,700

Population 465 | Est. 1924

The burn ban in Texas has nothing to do with drought and everything to do with the noxious gas seeping from the oil wells that pockmark the landscape. If I struck a match, my tent could rocket so high in the air I could maybe see Antarctica. For most of my life I was annoyed by environmentalists—I was scared of what many had to say, so I marginalized them in my head. But I want this world to have a future. I want to have kids who aren't punished for the behavior of those who came before them. I want to stop smelling those noxious fumes.

John Steinbeck said, "Once you are in Texas it seems to take forever to get out, and some people never make it." I was fine with the "take forever" part, but the "never make it" haunted me. A man in his early nineties pulled up in a white pickup wearing a red checkered shirt, big hearing aids, and a John Deere hat.

"Where you headin'?" he asked.

"California," I said curtly. The suspicion in his eye kept me from explaining any more voluntarily. He wanted to play a part and I let him.

"California, huh? People around this county like to know who's passin' through it and what their destination is."

I looked around and saw only the skeletal remnants of recently plowed cotton fields for miles in every direction. Those people must be hiding, I thought. I turned around to let him read my pack. In two seconds he was done reading—which means he probably didn't read it.

"Well, okay then. You take care," he said, pulling a gold star from his breast pocket. "I'm a deputy in this county." His voice carried a not-so-subtle warning that made me wonder if he thought I had plans to smuggle a giant crop sprinkler out of the state—the only thing within sight that I could harm or potentially steal.

"That's good to know," I said.

"All right then," he said and drove off.

A few miles down the road, Sheriff Wallace Stalcup, who was in his early seventies and wore a tan cowboy hat, pulled over and said, "Where you heading?" I told him.

"What you're doing is a good thing. Pat Tillman, is for lack of a better word, a hero. Do you need anything?"

I said, "How far is Bledsoe from here?"

"Awhile yet for you. Maybe six miles."

"Well, if you have any water, I could use a bit."

"I don't have any, but the people in Bledsoe are sure to fill your bottles if you knock on their door." We shook hands and he drove off.

Twenty minutes later he pulled next to me again. "I couldn't get you out of my mind. Give me those water bottles." He took them and drove twelve miles round-trip to fill them. He returned, handed them over, and, with tears in his eyes, said, "What Pat did for our country is one of the bravest, most admirable things I can remember anyone doing. Take this for your cause." He gave me a hundred dollars.

I said, "Wow. That is extremely generous of you. Thank you."

"It is absolutely nothing compared to what he gave for our country. I'm embarrassed not to give you more."

"Sometimes I think this country requires too much from us."

"It's a harsh world. With a lot of evil people out there."

"Yeah, but—"

"I hope the rest of your journey is a safe one."

I thanked him again and he drove off. I slept under an old-time windmill eight miles from Tatum.

8

New Mexico

I was on a never-ending ribbon of road, walking above a calm ocean of moonlit dust, as I entered my favorite state. There were no flashing red radio towers, tall white windmills, or glowing orange streetlights. It was dark.

My sophomore year in high school, my dad took me out of school for a two-week road trip. He was looking for work in California. My teachers weren't pleased. I was excited but anxious about my dad's rejection of routine and order and happily agreed to escape from school. We slept in the car mostly. One of those nights was under a full moon surrounded by distant New Mexican plateaus on a quiet side road in the dessert. I grew restless trying to sleep in the passenger seat that night and rolled out of the car onto the side of the road as soon as I heard my dad snoring. I used a coat as my pillow and fell asleep on the hard, pebble-strewn ground, staring at the moon. I fell in love with New Mexico that night.

In the military we jumped into the White Sands military base—where the geography most resembled Afghanistan—on a clear November night. They strapped a giant rocket launcher to me. The weight of the long green ceramic pipe pulled me head-first out of the plane. The parachute opened and sliced a two-inch gap in my chin. I landed and chin skin flapped like an unmasted sail in the warm, dark desert wind. I hardly noticed the blood pouring from my face because I was so happy to be back in New Mexico, with a few moments to reflect and briefly escape the military's attempt to lobotomize me. My squad leader—in Afghanistan I would later see him running around lost in the sound of rocket fire, doing everything but leading—barked when he saw me: "Hey, John Wayne, buckle your fucking chin strap. I don't care how much you're bleeding." I liked the solitude of New Mexico.

A supersonic aircraft rattled the rocks on the road as I walked with my pack alone through my tenth state that night. The government had chosen Los Alamos, which was only a few miles from me, as the site for the Manhattan project. How did the place where I could see myself the clearest in also become the birthplace of the atomic bomb? New Mexico, my favorite secret spot, was also the military's favorite secret spot. I walked until almost one in the morning, hoping to find cell reception and trying to conserve water.

I felt like I was chasing chickens as a frantic wind blew coats, bags, hats, and my tent across a cow pasture while I attempted to pack the next morning. Soon after, a fire-hose stream of air kept me fighting to maintain a pace of less than a mile and a half per hour. It was the most challenging wind of the trip. I visualized myself as a cheese wire, cutting thin and sharp through the invisible pressure. When that grew dull I chased my hat brim as if it were a plastic rabbit at the dog track. *The next time I walk across the country I'll start at the Pacific and walk with the wind,* I thought. For hours the wind continued to yell "No!" until finally, around six, the great Western throat grew hoarse and the sun, the stirred dust, and the metallic clouds calmed into a well-beaten-bruise color in the sky. Any other state, and my staff and I would have been irritated by the treatment. I saw that day, however, as a rite of passage into New Mexico. I thought that I would endure months like that to earn New Mexico's respect.

TATUM, NM | Mile 1,757

Population 683 | Est. 1909

A wind advisory with forty-mile-an-hour gusts turned Tatum and Highway 380 into a blurry and indiscernible Russell Chatham landscape painting. I saw a man with rust-colored hair and ripped jeans sitting on a pallet under an underpass. He stared at the ground and didn't notice I was walking toward him. He looked up and I was standing over him. I handed him the hundred dollars the sheriff had given me. I left without words being exchanged.

I was seventy-five service-free miles from the nearest town: no gas stations or restaurants until Roswell. Water was the bulk of the challenge. I added seven pounds of water weight to my pack. The extra weight, heavy winds, and length of time until my next refueling kept me in Tatum waiting for better wind. Kevin Tillman called me that night. It had been years since we'd last talked. He said he was inspired by what I was doing; he said Pat would be proud. The call rekindled a friendship that has lasted to this day. Kevin is one of the most genuine people I know.

He is also one of the most courageous people I know. He spoke truth to power before Congress when he demanded answers and accountability of those who covered up Pat's death. Before Congress and the nation, he eloquently said:

> In the days leading up to Pat's memorial service, media accounts based on information provided by the Army and the White House were wreathed in a patriotic glow and became more dramatic in tone. A terrible tragedy that might have further undermined support for the war in Iraq was transformed into an inspirational message that served instead to support the nation's foreign policy wars in Iraq and Afghanistan. To further exploit Pat's death, he was awarded the Silver Star for valor. . . . It's a bit disingenuous to think that the administration did not know about what was going on, something so politically sensitive.[23]

You don't hear such candor on TV very often, especially from someone testifying before Congress. There was no double talk or tiptoeing around the truth during Kevin's testimony. You certainly didn't hear the same candor from Donald Rumsfeld or the generals called to testify about the cover-up. Kevin said it like it was.

I was in Montana at a bar on May 30, 2004, when I heard that Pat's death had been a friendly-fire incident. ESPN had nearly twenty-four-hour coverage of the story. An angry but determined feeling settled into me that day. I soon challenged myself to figure out what other lies I was being fed. I vowed not to let the news of the cover-up poison me with cynicism and apathy. I couldn't. The military and the government had taken enough energy from me. They wouldn't take any more.

So I set out to really learn. But that's easier said than done. It's hard to say you're going to figure out how the system works and do your best to take ownership over this country and expose injustices when you have to worry about paying the bills. Like Caleb, the little boy behind the register in Paris, Texas, said, "You can't change the world until the mortgage is paid."

Many of my family and friends rejected the way the Tillman family confronted the military. Accidents happened, they said. The powers that be were doing their best. The fact is, the system worked for most of my family and friends. They lived in good homes. They believed they had earned all of what they had and that those who hadn't needed to stop being lazy and blaming others for their dependence on the government—that, somehow, those who had none of the military, political, or economic power were the ones responsible for all the problems. Questioning my family and friends' beliefs meant risking my relationship with them. They helped me learn how to stand up for what I believed in. But Pat and Kevin made figuring out the truth and holding the powers that be accountable feel necessary and important—even if the price was high.

Tatum is a small town. Noise pollution on Main Street amounts to the constant roll of wind chimes. There are three restaurants. One is in a gas station; the other is closed on both Sunday and Saturday. I ate at the third, the Steak House Cafe, three times. Twice someone paid for my meal without reading my pack or mentioning the walk. The townspeople knew who I was and what I was doing less than twelve hours after I arrived.

Metal art is the main tourist attraction in Tatum. From street to restaurant signs, thin metal silhouettes of Indians, aliens, soldiers, and coyotes ornament Tatum's frontage. There are two motels. One is condemned and the other is the Sands, where I stayed, which embraces a seventies-era motif. Its lack of pretension gives it a relaxing energy. The manager is Carla, who lives at the motel. She had managed it for ten years. She told me that she and her late husband had a handshake agreement with the man who held the note on the property. They were making payments to one day buy the Sands. The note holder decided to sell to a third party instead, and Carla was heartbroken. With tears rolling down her cheeks, she said, "This place is my ministry. I spread God's word here. I will be so sad to leave it." Carla donated the cost of room and did my laundry without charge. The next day, when we chatted, the tears had stopped and she seemed optimistic about the future. She had plans to move into a mobile home with her new husband and hoped to continue her ministry in a new way. She said, "I want to hand out grocery gift certificates to people I can sense need them."

Loaded with two boxes of cookies-and-cream Pop-Tarts, beef jerky, four tuna packets, eight quarts of water, and B vitamins, I left Tatum at noon for the seventy-three-mile town- and service-free walk to Roswell. The first six miles were slow. Then I noticed a wind hitting my back at a forty-five-degree angle, a rare and unfamiliar feeling walking west. It lasted an hour, during which I covered almost five miles in spite of my loaded pack. This propelled me into the night. The mile markers began to fall off like tin cans at pistol range. I had my head down and I was feeling good. Around ten-thirty that night I thought I would make a run at fifty. My previous best was 38.1.

I thought fifty was possible after I learned that the 101st Airborne Division had walked 150 miles in three days while training for World War II. Eisenhower—who as president would later go on to overthrow the democratically elected presidents of three sovereign countries—created the controversial and dangerous parachute division to catch the Germans off guard behind their lines. He knew the men of the 101st could get scattered and be forced to survive and walk on their own for days. Each "Screaming Eagle" hopeful had to walk 150 miles in seventy-two hours as part of the training. If they could do 150 in three days, I could try 50.

Highway 380 grew dark and quiet. Around two-thirty in the morning, popped semi tires began to look like squirming eels, road signs turned to axe murderers, and a lone mid-eighties white Buick abandoned on the side of the road was surely filled with drug dealers who would rob me of my dirty laundry. At three-thirty, after thirteen and a half hours of constant walking, I was suspiciously blissful. I had not seen a headlight in hours. A hazy moon was above me, New Mexico desert to my right and left. I was walking centered over the yellow-striped median, listening to Radiohead's "How to Disappear Completely." It seemed to have been written for me at that moment. The time before sunrise was the most difficult. My body felt old and broken. My forty-five-pound pack felt like a cancerous growth. I was paranoid from a lack of sleep. I was talking to myself and didn't want to walk ever again. The sun rose and I found a new burst of energy—only six miles to fifty. Those six miles took three hours. Finally, at ten a.m., I crossed the fifty-mile marker.

There are As to be made on tests, trophies to be won in sports, and well-earned paychecks to be received in the workforce. Walking fifty miles with a forty-five to fifty-five-pound pack on my back was an accolade-free accomplishment that meant as much to me as all of the above combined. At ten-thirty I climbed a fence and took a nap. The lactic acid that had pooled in my muscles made getting comfortable impossible. After a little stretching I fell asleep for forty-five minutes. I woke to thirty brown quarter horses staring at me. I stood up and they scattered. I slept the rest of the day and into the next morning. I was twenty-three miles from Roswell.

I climbed atop a plateau I had been staring at for twenty miles and saw white billows in the sky that were not clouds. It was my first glimpse of the snow-covered Rocky Mountains. Helping celebrate the milestone, scores of antelope jogged within thirty yards of me as I made my way down towards the city limits of Roswell, still worn down from the previous day's walk.

ROSWELL, NM | Mile 1,829

Population 48,366 | Est. 1869

At noon I met with Mark, the photographer for the *Roswell Daily Gazette*. We toured the UFO museum together. I have never been an alien-abduction enthusiast. I read and was scared by the book *Communion* when I was a teenager and sometimes listened to Art Bell interview "abductees" on his late-night radio show, but that was the extent and depth of my interest. I am sure life exists outside of our solar system and I'd love to see a UFO hover above me one night. Until then, I'm happy to spend my time learning as much as I can about the occupants of this planet.

Six-year-old Elijah Mendez was with his parents, Robert and Tracey, at Mama Tucker's Cakes and Donuts in Roswell the next morning. Elijah had recently undergone a successful bone-marrow transplant. His sister was a perfect match donor, and Elijah's leukemia was in remission. New Mexico does not have the capacity to treat pediatric bone-marrow patients, so the Mendez family had to fly to California. Because the procedure would take place out of state their insurance would not cover the five-million-dollar cost. It wasn't until the wife of a New Mexico senator advocated on the family's behalf that the insurance company came through. Hospital and hotel stays totaled two million dollars, the transplant cost one million, and the drugs another two million.

Elijah glowed with happiness. When I asked him what his name was, he said, "My name is Elijah from the Bible."

"Was that you the Bible was talking about?"

"No, I just have the same name."

I asked him what he wanted to do when he grows up. He said, "Be a veterinarian." He showed me a large mechanism taped to his chest that regulated his marrow. I told him it reminded me of *Transformers*. Elijah had won a "distinguished patient" award in the hospital for undergoing long radiation procedures without moving. Most adults and nearly all children require sedation during such procedures. Elijah didn't. He gave me five dollars for the Foundation and hugged me three different times.

For the first time all trip, I fell under the weather. I had a small fever and head cold. This combined with the forty-degree rain and a forecast of snow that night, kept me indoors at a cheap motel. I had spent about $2,500 up until that point of the walk. So many people had taken care of me. I felt like I could afford it. I was 999 miles from Los Angeles; I had raised about $35,000 for the Foundation.

When I took off again, it looked as if the Rocky Mountains had collapsed. With blue skies above and behind me, enormous puffs of smoky clouds rolled low in the horizon and obstructed my western view. Spring birds were chirping, green buds covered the limbs of trees and the sweet, light smell of high and dry altitude was all around me. It was hard to believe I had spent the fall and nearly all winter walking outside. Two twentysomethings with heavily starched baseball hats pulled over and handed me a brand new gallon of Lipton iced tea. It was the only human interaction I had all day.

I descended a six-degree grade for almost two miles as the sun set. I found myself in a canyon where rock faces and steep slopes rose to skyscraper heights. I could smell and hear a river. Stars were my only light. I was waiting to be ambushed by a hoard of treasure-seeking spirits from centuries past who had established the high ground. Billy the Kid had traveled this canyon; his ghost probably roamed here. He was considered a local hero, a Robin Hood figure, according to my sources in Roswell. Walking on the shoulder of the road on the canyon floor, I was sure to catch a few lonely night drivers off guard as their headlights reflected off my hunched back and cane in the darkness. I could almost hear doors lock as the cars drove by. I had a few opportunities to crawl into abandoned sheds for cover that night. No way. I was too scared. I would never dream of it. I would rather have mountain lions crawl in my tent than sleep in an abandoned shed in the wilderness. There is something horrifying about an abandoned man-made structure at night.

I camped atop a dome with the dark silhouettes of mountains encircling me. If a star existed, I could see it. I was in the most beautiful camping spot on the walk—partly because it had taken me six months to get there. There was not a light to be seen; other than a few deer, I was completely alone. I hadn't had cell reception in hours. Staring at all those constellations, I could make no sense of the shapes or names of the few I knew. The top eighth-grade public-school art students from every nation should meet in Switzerland one summer and rename the constellations. Why should the ancient Greeks own the night sky? It would be a great way to reengage the world with the stars. If more people spent time under an unobstructed night sky, we would be less sure of ourselves—which could be a good thing.

HONDO, NM | Mile 1,876

Population 1,081 | Est. 1880

Joe owns the Tangle Y Wood and Art Shop in Hondo, New Mexico. He and his girlfriend Stella saw me in the paper and invited me to stay at his home, thirty yards from the shop. Over dinner Stella said, "I was born in Mexico and married a coyote—the guides who take immigrants across the border for a price. He abused me. I couldn't leave my own home for seventeen years. I wondered if I would wake up dead some mornings. My husband was finally arrested in a drug bust and deported. I was left alone to raise my three kids, but I was finally free. Soon after, I went to work for Joe building cabinets."

Joe said, "She was the most trustworthy and hardest-working employee I ever hired. Now I stay out of her kitchen and she leaves the heavy lifting to me."

Stella cooked ribs, mashed potatoes, and cherry pie for us that night. Joe hunts every type of game there is, travels to places like Alaska on gold-mining expeditions, and specializes in the art of self-sufficiency. From building furniture and homes to gathering food, he does his best to do as much for himself as possible.

I had learned early on in the walk that people can't wait to tell you all the best things they have done in their life. If you show them your cool thing, they will show you theirs. There are a lot of amazing stories in the United States. Everyone seems to have one.

WHITE SANDS, NM | Mile 1,961

Population 1,323 | Est. 1941

The altitude drop into Carrizozo made for quick miles. I walked eighteen in a little over five hours. At noon I watched two men on horseback attempt to lasso a cow scooting across an expansive ranch. When they finally had it cornered, the 1,200-pound black bathtub hopped a four-strand barbed-wire fence like it was a white-tail. The lead cowboy threw his Stetson in frustration and I laughed.

I slept on the Valley of Fires lava flow. A volcano had erupted a thousand years ago seven miles north of where I set up camp. The lava stretched forty-four miles long and three miles wide. It resembled dreadlocks. The ropy lava is called *pahoehoe* in the Hawaiian language. I looked through my tent, trying to imagine people's real-time reactions to the eruption. It was surely a major cultural event that inspired fresh mythology. In a time without electric lights, the orange lava must have lit up the night sky and perhaps froze the social energy of the day when it cooled. Did the

Mescalero Apache lose any lives? Did they know what the lava was? Did they take it personally?

The next day I started walking through the White Sands missile range, a sixty-six-mile stretch of uninhabited land. From what I was told, the base was well guarded. That night, under all the stars and in an exhausted trance, I walked and listened to Radiohead's "Subterranean Homesick Alien." Then the earth shook. The loudest booms I had heard in years buckled my knees. I was grateful for my staff. The major explosions went on for hours. In my tent, I could hear the unnerving whooping sound of blacked-out helicopters unloading heavy machine-gun fire. They were so close I could almost touch them. I wondered if they saw me. I wasn't *in* White Sands, technically; I was across the street, hoping I would be fine. I covered almost twenty-seven miles that day. Twenty-seven miles over big hills feels like fifty over flat land. I wanted the machines to settle down.

The entire span of White Sands is a GPS dead spot. Bingham, New Mexico, the first town west of the Trinity site, is a town of three people and one rock shop. Reluctantly, I stopped in to fill my water bottles; I was expecting the water to be contaminated. I met Medicine Wolf and Shahawain (Choctaw for "white buffalo calf"). They were passing through on their way to a powwow in honor of the first day of spring. Medicine Wolf, a big man in his mid-fifties with unusually large hands, had heard of me and introduced himself. He and Shahawain were organizing an ecologically friendly community outside of Alamogordo. Their mantra was, "Simple is free." Medicine Wolf gave me a crystal he carried in his medicine bag, along with three months' worth of a special herbal blend to keep my immune system strong. He showed me how to focus my "third eye" using the circle stone I'd received as a gift in Walhalla, Georgia. He was surprised I was unaware of the "big medicine" I carried with me. He said, "Rory, your aura is full and green." I said it was because I was Irish. We exchanged contact information and I told them I would visit their community one day.

Trinity Site Nuclear Testing

The first atomic bomb test took place July 16, 1945, two months and eight days after the Germans surrendered. US propaganda films credit Albert Einstein's warning letter to Franklin Roosevelt—which urged the president to develop the bomb before the Germans did—as the impetus for the nuclear weapons program. Einstein would later regret sending the letter, saying, "Had I known that the Germans would not succeed in producing an atomic bomb, I would have never lifted a finger." But the US wasn't going to let the German surrender become a missed opportunity to try out the weapon it had spent two billion dollars and four years developing. The Russians had just invaded Japan, and the US scrambled to get the bomb over there before the Japanese surrendered. Japan had nearly run out of rice and hadn't been able to feed its soldiers or its population adequately throughout the previous year—you can't fight a war if the soldiers are starving.

On August 6, 1945, less than a month after the first test at the Trinity site, the "Little Boy," an untested uranium model of the A-bomb, was dropped on Hiroshima. It killed seventy thousand people and destroyed sixty thousand of the ninety thousand buildings in the city. Surviving parents woke to find their children buried and screaming under immovable burning rubble. Other survivors prayed for water as the skin melted off their bodies. Their prayers were answered: a short time after the bomb was dropped, it began to rain. People opened their mouths to catch the liquid that fell from the sky. But the rain turned into irradiated smoke- and ash-colored fluid that poisoned those who drank it. Thousands had their white-blood-cell production effectively turned off; their bodies began to rot from the inside out. The scientists who developed the bomb claimed not to have known this would be an effect of their experiment over Hiroshima.

Three days later the US wanted to test out its "Fat Man" plutonium implosion-style bomb over Nagasaki. It killed forty thousand people and destroyed most of Nagasaki's infrastructure, despite significantly missing its intended target and landing in a valley outside of the city. The US would drop another bomb over the Bikini Atoll eleven months later. This test displaced hundreds of Bikini natives and exposed thousands of American servicemen to cancerous radiation. By 1998 the US had tested 1,032 nuclear bombs, most of which dwarfed the first four tests.

SAN ANTONIO, NM
Mile 2,065

Population 165 | unincorporated

When looking for a place to sleep, climb a hill, if possible. It was my new rule of thumb. The extra effort was always worth it. Other than a smattering of orange light outlining the town of Socorro six miles to my north, I had a perfect view of the sky and peace of mind knowing I wouldn't be caught off guard. Although I enjoyed the landscapes of White Sands, I was happy to be out. Counting on Pop-Tarts and beef jerky to get me through the high desert made for a long few days, and thinking of the atomic bomb was depressing. The people at the Owl Café and the gas station covered my purchases. I was still surprised at such gestures even though I had received hundreds of them over the course of the prior seven months. The small-town business owners and workers who can least afford to donate are the most consistent donors.

SOCORRO, NM | Mile 2,075

Population 9,105 | Est. 1815

I climbed uphill against an endless avalanche of wind. Seventy-foot rock faces stood to my left and right. It wasn't a four-legged bear-crawl ascent, but it was steeper than any slope in the Appalachians. Little things irritated me that day. I saw a Styrofoam coffee cup on the side of the road and felt repulsed. I comforted myself with the imaginary sound of rickety wagon wheels and clanging soup ladles and envisioned short, thin pioneers with mustaches, bonnets, and itchy, weighty clothes making the same climb, only with less stable footing. I had spent the night in Socorro, founded in 1598. *Socorro* means "help" or "aid," so named after the Piro Pueblo people provided much needed food to the Spanish as they traveled through the area. In 1680 Socorro was destroyed during the Pueblo Revolt. The tension from heavy drought and famine, compounded by the decision of the Spanish government to hang three medicine men for practicing a mode of spirituality outside the Catholic teaching, spurred the uprising.

MAGDALENA, NM | Mile 2,092

Population 938 | Est. 1884

I always appreciate a city limit sign that greets me with an elevation rather than a population. Magdalena sits at 6,353 feet. The town's main water pump had broken the day before I entered the town. All restaurants and cafés were shut down. My only option was a Conoco gas station. I sat in an uncomfortable chair next to an electric outlet, ate a burrito, charged my phone, and watched a woman in her late sixties with a fake red alligator purse and short black hair play a five-dollar scratch-off game at least fifteen times. She came back into the store twice, each time with a handful of fresh cash. Conoco looked like Pompeii when she finally left for good, with a thick layer of scratch-off dust covering the gumball machines and ice-cream freezer. It was heartbreaking.

The lack of water had the small town buzzing. As people stood in line to pay for gas I heard, "With no water there is no shower, no toilet, no cooking, no cleaning. When will they have it fixed?" "I don't know. Some are saying tomorrow, others are saying in a week." I felt their pain. Filling up my water bottles with Dasani felt like paying for a can of fresh air. Fortunately, I was used to going to the bathroom outside and washing my hands with baby wipes. I left Magdalena earlier than I hoped to find a good tree outside the city limits. I was sure this mineral-rich old cattle town with a few interesting-looking art galleries was wonderful once you got to know her.

I soon experienced the questionable grandeur of the Very Large Array, situated fifteen miles east of Datil, New Mexico. Carl Sagan wrote about this Y-shaped crop of radio telescopes in the book *Contact*. The VLA sits in a dry lake bed and is surrounded by silent mountains that seem to look incredulously at the telescopes. With all the wars, poverty, sectarianism, and inequality in the world, I thought, you'd think we would try to communicate better with each other before we bother with extraterrestrials. It took me three hours to walk across the Very Large Array. As the daylight grew dimmer, I realized that all of the twenty-five antennae—that I could count—were following the setting sun in unison. The telescopes began to resemble innocent street kids looking for a little security, guidance, or maybe even an adoption from a passing tourist. They looked lonely.

DATIL, NM | Mile 2,127

Population 54 | Est. 1885

Datil's grocery store, gas station, bar, and motel are all the same place. The uncommonly large elk heads hanging in the few rooms looked prehistoric. I walked into a severe headwind to get there. Forty-five minutes after I arrived, the snow began to fall. I watched the blizzard through a log-framed window in front of a blackened stone fireplace that would have fit well in a medieval British castle. I was seventy-eight miles from Arizona and thought I would savor the few remaining miles of New Mexico by staying the night. I wished there was more to document but the 150 residents were at home and the grocery store/bar/diner/motel was empty.

CONTINENTAL DIVIDE

I camped on the Continental Divide. If I had been sliced down the middle that night, half of my blood would have drained to the Atlantic and the other half to the Pacific. The Divide is obvious, yet unpredictable. Some areas look like the Cliffs of Dover; at other points wind erosion has carved out stone towers; in less dramatic areas, giant knuckles of tree-covered hill mark the route. Highway 60 crosses the Divide at 7,800 feet. I forced myself well off the road and up the steep and sandy back end of a four-hundred-foot sheer rock face. The thin air nearly drowned me.

I hurried because I wanted to see the sun set. When I made it to the top, I kept turning in circles. Every degree offered a distant and well-contoured view. I sat at the edge of a cliff and watched the sun set imagining people on vision quests sitting in the same spot throughout the centuries, marveling at our shared view. I thought of the words of Alan Watts: "Through our eyes, the universe is perceiving itself. Through our ears, the universe is listening to its harmonies. We are the witnesses through which the universe becomes conscious of its glory, of its magnificence."

I felt the urge to follow the Divide south, toward warmth. I wanted to stay connected to this sublime and ancient feeling. I watched the stars intently that night, staring out through the opening of my tent, under a giant bush that blocked the wind.

PIE TOWN, NM | Mile 2,148

Population 2,900 | Est. 1920

Green chilies and piñons in apple pie? Only in Pie Town, New Mexico. I would have never dreamed those two ingredients would be the decisive factor in what is quite possibly the most complex, intense, and best-tasting dessert I have had. Pie Town was given its name by Clyde Norman, who liked to bake dried apple pie and began selling pies to travelers along Highway 60 near the Arizona line in the 1920s. Kathy and her mom visited Pie Town thirteen years before I arrived and were surprised to see that no one had sold pie since Clyde. They decided to buy and refurbish one of the three buildings in town and specialize in the sale of pies. Investing her savings in a business eighty-five miles from the closest reasonably sized city (Socorro) was a big gamble. But, Kathy told me, she had faith in the notion that "if you do what you love, make the best pies in the universe, and treat people well, they will come, regardless of how remote the location." Using her grandmother's recipes, Pie-o-neer (the name of Kathy's café) has attracted the Food Network and *Travel and Leisure* magazine and won *Sunset* magazine's "best pie in the West" for its coconut cream pie. The restaurant was brimming with cross-country travelers.

Kathy gives all of her recipes away for free when asked. "The more people there are in the world who can make good pie, the better off the world will be." With contagious enthusiasm, she sat at my table and introduced me to customers, employees, and her boyfriend Stan, who helped run the place. Stan snapped at someone who came into use the bathroom but didn't buy any food. "I'll take a dollar for that toilet paper you just used," he said to an embarrassed woman who dropped her eyes and pretended like she didn't hear as she left the restaurant. Stan went on: "People come in here and use the bathroom like it doesn't cost us 200 miles in gas money to bring the toilet paper out here. I'm tired of it." I spent three hours at the cafe talking about pies, astronomy, the dangers of a computerized ballot system (Stan thought it was a recipe for corruption), the life stories of three different couples who were traveling through town (they were from New York, North Carolina, and Los Alamos, New Mexico), the Pat Tillman Foundation, and the secrets to a happy life. It's easy to talk about the secrets to a happy life when you're eating pie.

QUEMADO, NM | Mile 2,170

Population 250 | Est. 1880

A snowstorm hit around five in the morning. After saving the roof of my tent from collapsing, I packed up and began to walk. I soon looked like a Siberian yak as my overgrown beard became glazed with snow and ice. I was only six miles from Quemado and was warm before I knew it. I met Mike, the owner of the local grocery store. He was the third person I met who brought up wolves that week. The Mexican gray wolf was reintroduced to the state by the US Fish and Wildlife Service in 1998, after it was wiped out by ranchers in the 1920s. Since then, New Mexico's wolf population increased exponentially. The elk and livestock that spent the last eighty years free from the burden of the wolf have become easy prey. Mike explained that the wolves have figured out how to use barbed-wire fences to corner elk calves—and now the elk population is being decimated.

"You may shoot a wolf only if it is consuming livestock. If it is killing a pet, you have to let it. I asked a game warden if my three-year-old daughter was safe walking around our property. The game warden said, 'Probably.' Then he said, 'Oh, wait, do you have dogs?' I said, 'Yes.' He said, 'Be careful.'" Mike went on to add, "There are a lot of people around here that see the wolf as a biological weapon designed to run us off the land we have worked for generations. Let me tell you: it's working."

Because I climb barbed-wire fences most nights to camp, it is always in the back of my mind I will wake to someone saying, "Hey, this is private property. Get off my land," while charging the barrel of a shotgun. That night was one of the rare occasions where I was certain not to be bothered. I built a large cedarwood fire to celebrate. I was alone and twenty-two miles from Arizona.

The last five miles of New Mexico were the most beautiful. The road ran straight and flat down the center of two merging plateaus as the sun set into Arizona. At many borders it is hard to tell where one state ends and the other begins. Here, though, there was an unmistakable natural checkpoint, with the rock formations acting as noble and even-tempered guards. They thanked me for my business and helped me count the last of the single-digit mile markers. And like it had my first day in New Mexico, when I'd made my way past the state's windy security system into Tatum, the wind pushed up against me once more—only this time, I like to think, it was stirred by a reluctance to let me leave. I slept on the New Mexico side of the state line. If I was attacked by a mountain lion, I decided, I would roll across the border in my sleeping bag so I could say I made it as far as Arizona. But I would roll back to New Mexico before breathing my last breath. It was the state I would prefer to die in.

It was April and I was in Arizona. I saw two elk cows that afternoon. They carried themselves like heirs to the throne of the animal kingdom and let me walk within fifty yards of them before running off to high tea.

9

Arizona

SPRINGERVILLE, AZ | Mile 2,219

Population 1,961 | Est. 1948

> *Most personalities have been obliged to be rebels. Half their strength has been wasted in friction. . . . The note of the perfect personality is not rebellion, but peace.*
>
> —**Oscar Wilde,** *The Soul of Man under Socialism*

I entered Arizona thinking, for some reason, of Tomeka from the Quick Stop back in Arkansas. "I wish I had more time to think. I have too much responsibility to do what you are doing," she had said. Was this walk a way of avoiding the type of responsibility Tomeka was talking about? Was I growing scared of the thought of going back to twenty-first-century life as I crossed the border of my second-to-last state? The people who caused the crash of 2008 were already trying to deflect the blame onto the poor and cutting the budgets of programs that served them. Would we all have to start working harder for less to pay the debts of the rich? Was this what I was walking toward—

the decision between rolling over to be exploited or fighting for radical changes to the system? I didn't like either option. This sense of the end caused me to take in less during the day. I started to feel less philosophical; my blog entries became shorter.

To control the fear of losing the freedom and support I felt during the walk, I tried to stop enjoying it so much—if it was all going to burn out, it would be a controlled burn.

Three days before I entered the military I had shaved my head, something I knew they were going to do for me. If I was going to be reborn into a world of harsh discipline and control, I would beat them to it. I would show that I was still aware of what was happening to me, not just along for the ride. A small personal rebellion, but cathartic nonetheless.

I walked into a grand buffet of land formations my first day in Arizona: snow-brushed mountains, river-cut canyons, rolling hills, and plateaus long enough to land a 747 on. The wind was back and violent as ever. Local residents told me that Springerville—elevation seven thousand feet—is the windiest town in the United States.

I entered the offices of the *White Mountain Independent* and met Karen, the only person sitting in the unfurnished newsroom, and asked her if she wanted to do a story on the walk. She brewed some green tea with ink-stained fingers and said, "I focus on 'human-interest' stories and avoid politics and mainstream media obsessions like corruption, crime, and disaster if I can." I wondered how she kept the paper going. She was excited to do a story on the walk.

As we talked, Ron Kessler walked in the office with the late afternoon sun and said, "Do you know where I can find Rory Fanning?" Karen pointed me out.

Ron wore a white fleece with a fish skeleton on it. "Hi, Rory! I tracked you down through your blog. I knew stopping in at the paper would be a good idea. I never thought I'd find you this soon, though! I'm traveling to see my family in Phoenix from Denver. I've searched the Internet for fellow cross-country walkers. You're one of the few who are actually serious about it. I walked from the Atlantic to the Pacific last year for breast cancer awareness. My first girlfriend passed away from it a while back and I wanted to raise money for research. I don't want to interrupt your interview, but I did want to stop in and say hi."

I was surprised by his ability to find me as well. I wrapped up my conversation with Karen, who invited me to stay at her house—I gladly accepted—and then sat down with Ron to talk about gear and the logistics of walking through the Arizona desert. Ron offered to scout out the rest stops on my route to Tempe so I could carry the right amount of water. We both appreciated the backbreaking burden of the extra water weight necessary for a seventy-mile walk across a barren stretch of land. He also said, "When you get back to normal life and need someone to talk with about the transition, be sure to call me. Working and walking for a cause you believe in every day obviously gives you a strong sense of purpose. You might feel a little deflated when you get home."

"Kind of like Meriwether Lewis?" I replied.

"What did he do?"

I said with a chuckle, "He disemboweled himself with a shard of glass after his journey." Ron raised his eyebrows in a look of surprise. I was embarrassed by my comment.

"I doubt that's you. You've spent the better part of a year being consumed by small details. If you're anything like me, you thought your walk was about doing something big in the beginning, but soon learned it was about the small. Irritating shoulder straps, thousands of mile-marker signs, the stones in the asphalt, these are all the little things you have been forced to spend your day thinking about. You're going to see the world in a way you didn't before the walk. Even if you fall back into old routines, this experience will be etched in your brain. After my walk the little things became big and the big things little—I don't really feel the need to make a million dollars or win some big award right now. I'm doing my best to hold onto that. I doubt you will do anything as dramatic as Meriwether Lewis, I'm guessing he was addicted to the big things, and there is no peace in that. It seems to me that he missed the point of it all. A lot of people miss the point."

"Well, to be completely honest, I'm not looking forward to going back to the world and finding a real job . . ."

"Yeah, if you figure a way around that, let me know! I'm just glad we had a chance to connect. It's nice to meet another person who carried their shit across this country like I did. We need to stay in touch."

SHOW LOW, AZ | Mile 2,265

Population 7,695 | Est. 1870

After a steak dinner and a rest at Karen's house I set out for Show Low, birthplace of George Takei (the LGBTQ rights activist and actor, famous for his role as Hikaru Sulu in *Star Trek*). The town was named after a high-stakes poker game between C. E. Cooley and Marion Clark. The two decided there was only room in town for one of them. They agreed to let a game of cards decide who would leave. Clark said, "If you can show low, you win." Cooley flipped over the deuce of clubs (the lowest possible card) and replied, "Show low it is." Cooley took Clark's hundred-thousand-acre ranch. Clark was never heard from again. Show Low's main street is named Deuce of Clubs Street in honor of the event.

Karen from the paper picked me up again to stay at her house another night. She invited her psychic friend Tina over for a spaghetti dinner. Tina owned a metaphysical bookstore in Show Low. At dinner Tina regaled us with tales of her near-death experience and the spirits she met in her dreams.

"Four and a half years ago," Tina told us, "I was visited between seven and ten occasions by a man in my sleep. He was very mischievous and energetic in a playful, fun way. He and I spoke on a range of topics. I remember waking up giddy every morning because of the joy that emanated from him. I wish I could remember more of what we talked about. One of the things I do remember him saying was, 'I think I always sensed there was something bigger out there that couldn't be captured or truly understood in a church. I could never put my finger on it though. I had no idea it was this big!' He also wanted me to tell his family that he was okay. About a year later I saw a show, on PBS, I believe. I immediately recognized his eyes. It was the man who I spoke with in my dreams. I couldn't believe it. I never watch the news and did not know who Pat Tillman was until that PBS special. This is only the second time I've told this story."

"Why would he visit you out here in Show Low, Arizona?" I asked.

"There are certain people who act almost as street lights at night. A spirit can see that light and is led to it for one reason or another, mainly because they know they will be heard. I am one of many out there. I have gotten to a point in my life where I accept it," Tina said.

Before I left Karen and Tina, I received a skeletal adjustment by a chiropractor, Dr. Rick. He had served in the navy and liked helping veterans. Karen worked in his office as a reflexologist. She made the appointment, and he didn't charge me. My jaw was off-center and he said it was affecting my sinuses. Other than that there were no other issues with my alignment, which was surprising after nearly three thousand miles with a forty-five-pound pack.

I loved sleeping in a bed when given the chance, but I never missed one when I was wrapped in a sleeping bag in my tent. A long day of walking made any rest satisfying, like a starving person who is happy to eat bugs. I made a small fire atop a steep wooded area that had been burned in a major fire seven years ago. The fire, allegedly started by an out-of-work firefighter, attracted the international news media and displaced fifty thousand local residents. It was eerie sleeping in the charred remains of a once-green forest. I felt like I was camping in a cemetery, only none of the bodies were buried.

BLACK MESA, AZ | Mile 2,458

Population 0 | Est. at least 7,000 years ago

I was greeted by at least forty Black Mesa Hot Shots (BMHS) as I walked through Heber, Arizona, the next day. The BMHS are the Special Forces of the firefighting community. They respond to the most destructive national and international forest fires. Training is intense because they can be called to marathon firefighting missions, like one in California in 1987 where they were on shift for two separate forty-day tours. The following year they went to Yellowstone, near my dad's house, for another two thirty-day assignments. Then there was the Rodeo-Chediski fire that burned 230 homes in Heber-Overgaard, Arizona—the one started by an unemployed firefighter. The BMHS must be able to hike with heavy gear into remote sections of wilderness in iron-melting temperatures. They described a training that seemed as intense as Ranger training. "We don all our firefighting equipment in the blazing Arizona sun and carry fake bodies out of the forest," one of them said.

Another, who had hands big and strong enough to tear a phone book in half, said, "We sign up knowing fighting forest fires is one of the most dangerous jobs in the world. But we do it anyway to save lives, houses, and forest land."

"We also like the adrenaline rush and the sense of family we all share," said a third.

When I was in Roswell I had picked up a pair of forest-green cargo pants for ten dollars. The BMHS wear identical pants, so we all matched for the picture we took together. It was good to see that people could collectively organize to do something positive for society. I needed to see an example of that—the BMHS fought destruction, they didn't bring it.

That night I was back in the kind of dense pine forest I had grown to love back east, only now I could feel the eyes of elk on me. While I built my fire for coffee the next morning the wind was wrestling violently with itself, so I gathered the biggest stones

I could find to keep my flames contained. I lifted the last rock for the circle and found a shiny brown snake coiled in hibernation. It seemed as long as my staff. I wasn't scared of it. That morning, the stillness of the reptile was enviable. Rather than slamming the rock and jumping back, I stared at this thing and almost fell into a seasonal trance along with it. I wanted to be that snake, rather than worry about what I was going to do after I finished the walk, and for a fleeting second I was.

PAYSON, AZ | Mile 2,546

Population 15,601 | Est. 1973

The thirty miles down the Rim into Payson were exhausting and beautiful. Over that stretch, the elevation dropped from 7,500 to 5,000 feet. The walking-downhill muscles in my legs were the weakest. Descending, I stared at a spotless blue sky, distant mountains, and pine trees and thought about the past. On the shoulder of that quiet road, buried by time and earth, the area's history stared at me like a face without eyes. I Googled "Payson Rim Native Americans" and learned that the earliest inhabitants of Payson Rim Country had been the Mogollons, a tribe of people who moved to this location from what is now known as New Mexico in 300 B.C. They lived in and around the Payson Rim for 1,800 years, until they became the Pueblo and Hohokam tribes. The Mogollons lived in the area for nine times longer than the United States has existed. The Pueblos and Hohokams were soon absorbed into the Apaches—a blanket label for several culturally related tribes. Of the 2,300 years of Native American history in the area, I was ashamed to realize I'd heard the story of only one person: the character Tonto, from the TV show *The Lone Ranger. Tonto,* in Spanish, means "stupid" or "foolish."

Tracy, Tina's friend, drove lunch out to where I had been walking. She said she had spoken to her ex-husband Dean and he had an extra bedroom. He was willing to pick me up at the end of the day and let me sleep at his house. At six the next morning, I woke to a pounding on my bedroom door.

"Rory, get up! I want to take you somewhere before you leave!"

I was up and packing before Dean finished his sentence. I made lunch from the cold cuts in his fridge and we were off. Driving up toward snowy mountains, dense pine forests, and a placid, rock-strewn river in his white Thunderbird, Dean said, "There is a very important chapter of history few people take the time to consider. I am going to show you ruins that date back twelve hundred years, complete with petroglyphs and pottery."

Dean worked for the county and was responsible for maintaining and making the guideposts along the roads. He lived in a small but tidy house by himself. He watched Fox News and read *National Geographic*. He was reading a book about history's most excruciating torture techniques: honey and rats, boiling water, and burying people up to their neck in the desert after cutting off their eyelids were a few of the techniques he described. He had a son who was in the Marine Force Recon. His son was his favorite topic.

We also talked about politics.

"Small government is what we need," said Dean.

"I agree."

"Yeah, we work too hard to be taxed the way we are."

"Government is microscopic for the rich and quite bloated for the rest of us. We have more people in prison per capita than any other country in the world, but somehow no one who crashed the economy via Wall Street has made it there yet. Or it would be nice if the government spent a portion of the money they paid private companies to build our military on public schools." I was warming up.

"We need to get back to the Constitution." Dean said.

"The Constitution hasn't done a great job making sure you have a real voice when it comes to the direction of this country—you have to raise millions if you want to be a member of Congress, there's nothing democratic about that. The Constitution also watched approvingly over slavery, denied women the right to vote, and didn't blink as a handful of people created the largest national wealth divide in human history. What part of the Constitution do you think we should go back to?" I said.

"Yeah, well, I don't think we're gonna resolve this here."

"You're probably right."

Dean's job helped him learn the history and layout of the land surrounding his house. We traveled deep into the forest, where he showed me waterfalls, grazing deer, and the ruins. At the Shoofly Village ruins, pottery shards hid amongst tall shoots of grass, rocks, and stones and were scattered and broken into small pieces by elk and other animals. He pointed out enough pieces that I felt fine taking one of the thousands that littered the ground. Roughly 250 people once lived there in what anthropologists believe was an eighty-room compound. A stone wall still encircled the entire area.

Cochise

Cochise, born in 1805, was Gèronimo's father-in-law and served as chief of the Chokonen band of the Chiricahua Apaches.[24] He led an uprising against Americans that began in 1861 and was the last of the great chiefs to surrender to the US government. He eluded the cavalry for years.

Cochise spent much of his younger years in the Superstition Mountains, where Dean took me. Cochise's father, Dean told me, used to make him take a sip of water and hold it in his mouth without swallowing a drop, then send him running up and down a tall, steep mountain. I thought this was a simple rite of passage/torture technique until I tried it that day. Holding the water in your mouth forces you to stay focused on deep, proper breathing while under physical stress. Surprisingly, I felt calm and centered in a situation where I would otherwise be gasping for air. Dean continued, "One day Cochise was sent out to find two eagle feathers. So he killed a small animal and buried himself for four days in the sand as he fended off other predators who wanted to eat the meat. Finally an eagle swooped down to grab the dead animal and Cochise snagged two feathers from its tail." Cochise fought the colonizers gallantly for years until, finally, he concluded that it was in the best interest of his tribe to surrender. He was shackled to the back of a wagon and walked along almost the same route I traveled, ending in Florida, where many other Native people were sent to die. Cochise managed to escape the Florida swamps and followed the setting sun back to Arizona on foot. He was caught again—and sent to the circus as a trained animal.

MESA, AZ | Mile 2,621

Population 439,041 | Est. 1878

I was back at sea level and only a few dozen miles from Tempe. I found hundreds of saguaro cacti, prickly arms raised, surrendering to the dessert heat. The cactus is nicknamed "the old man in the desert" because it does not grow its first arm until it is 75 years old and can live to be more than 150—which means some of the cacti I saw may have watched their land be ceded to the United States after the Mexican-American War in 1848.

Karen and Tina were waiting for me thirty-five miles outside of Tempe, at a roadside pulloff. They had books and a full Easter lunch spread out on a portable picnic table behind Karen's Jeep. They had driven 130 miles down from Show Low so I could celebrate the day with caring faces. Neither of them was a devout Christian, but it was a spiritual day for them and they wanted to share that with me. There was a sweetness in the gesture that was as real as the food they had waiting for me. "There is truth in all religions," said Tina.

I declined two generous offers to stay the night in Phoenix so I could make up for a slow day of walking the day before. When I finally reached my goal mile marker for the day, I was at a landfill that burned my eyes and nose. A tall ceramic chimney lapped at the blue sky with its methane flame until the sky was a dark orange, I couldn't stop until I was upwind. Beat, I was forced to walk another two miles to escape the fumes.

Dusk is a time when most people's lives are shifting from public to private. Sleeping on the side of the road in a tent near or in a town, I lost the anticipation of privacy.

When I returned from the military, after long days at the bank, I used to take late-night summer runs, then jump into Lake Michigan and swim out as far as I could into the blackness. It was a frightening privacy I was looking for out in the bottomless water—a privacy like death. Its comforting solitude reminded me of my will to live in service of life.

TEMPE, AZ | Mile 2,628

Population 161,719 | Est. 1894

Waves of heat smothered my face and body as I made my way through Mesa into Tempe. My clothes were heavy with sweat and I was ready for a shower. I cleaned up at a motel and walked to the Pat Tillman Foundation. It felt like the Mecca of my seven-month walk. Pat Tillman's ASU and Cardinals jerseys, along with a few of the most famous photos of him, were framed and hung neatly in a modern office space. His Lott Trophy sat on a desk and a dozen pictures of past Pat's Runs—a 4.2-mile run in honor of Pat Tillman's jersey number 42—were on the wall near the entrance door. I met Sean, the director of development of the foundation; Katie, the new executive director; Suzanne, the operations director; and Shannon, the Pat's Run coordinator. All were excited for the run that Saturday. They were expecting close to twenty thousand people. I spoke at length with Sean, a handsome, dark-haired man. He had lost his wife on 9/11 and was so moved by Pat's decision that he left a high-profile job on Wall Street to help grow the Foundation. He said, "I won't rest until the Tillman Foundation is a national force in leadership development." He was the type of person

I was hoping to appeal to during the walk, someone who was willing to sacrifice his immediate material interests for the long-term health of humanity. He thought the Pat Tillman Foundation was a vehicle to do that.

That afternoon I gave an interview, then stopped by the ASU stadium to help fill goodie bags for the run. I stayed in Tempe for a week waiting for race day, where I would be the race-starter. Normally the job of pulling the trigger went to Bruce Snyder, Pat Tillman's coach at ASU, but he had just passed away. I spoke with him after he allowed me to stand in his place to present the Pat Tillman Award at the East-West Shrine Game. Our conversation, along with his weekly Caring Bridge blog posts, which gave personal updates on his battle with cancer, made it obvious that he was a man with deep compassion, a sense of humor, and a heroic spirit. When I heard the news of his passing I was sitting in a Taco Bell in Fountain Hills, Arizona, reading Dan Millman's *Way of the Peaceful Warrior*, which Karen had given me on Easter. Millman quoted George Bernard Shaw at the beginning of one of the chapters: "I want to be thoroughly used up when I die, for the harder I work the more I live. I rejoice in life for its own sake. Life is no 'brief candle' to me; it is a sort of splendid torch which I have got hold of for the moment, and I want to make it burn as brightly as possible."

I was honored but saddened by the opportunity to start the race.

During the week, Kevin Tillman arranged for me to speak to the Arizona State baseball team. It was the first time Kevin, Mary, and Pat Tillman Sr. would hear my talk. The thought of doing this was initially nerve-wracking, but there is a palpable strength that emanates from each member of the Tillman family. It was a strength that didn't make me feel small. It was a strength that emboldened me. Holding my staff, standing in front of the team, with black leather chairs in front of lockers that held bats, helmets, and maroon-and-gold uniforms, I repeated the same talk I had given dozens of times. Mary Tillman had tears in her eyes afterward, and the family seemed genuinely moved by what I was doing. I could see where Pat got the strength to speak his mind.

Mauri had been following the walk since Charlotte. His wife Cindy taught at Sunset Elementary and arranged for me to speak at her school while I was in Tempe. They have two boys, Jake, six, and Brady, five. Mauri had been a fan of Pat since his ASU days. He said, "It seems there is always an asterisk that follows celebrity. So-and-so was a great athlete or a talented person in such-and-such a way but he didn't pay his taxes, or had a problem with alcohol, or women, or something. There was never a *but* with Pat. Everyone spoke so highly of his character. That's why the Mesa/Tempe Valley had an extremely hard time with his death. It is so rare to see someone work as hard as he did and do it with uncompromising character and integrity. He should not have played college football. He should not have played in the NFL. But he relentlessly willed it for himself."

It was a wonderful week. I was happy to be donating and walking for the foundation that helped veterans with money for education in the name of an extraordinary person, but I was beginning to realize the limits of nonprofits. The world was better because the organization existed, but it was bound by the rules of a corrupt and broken national economic and political system. As much as I enjoyed the people at the Foundation and thought their work was important, I left Tempe knowing that nonprofits weren't going to provide the change the world needed following the crash of 2008.

PERRYVILLE MINIMUM SECURITY PRISON, AZ | Mile 2,659

Population 2,382 | Est. 1982

I held a microphone and my staff and stared at 350 women in orange jumpsuits in the "yard" of Perryville prison, thinking about change. In prison the routines are the same, the uniforms are the same, and the scenery stays the same for as long as you're stuck there.

The walk wasn't changing the world like I hoped, but I was changing. At one time I had thought there was such a thing as human nature—which was "fallen," like the Bible said, or selfish, in secular terms. I saw too much change in myself to believe in a fixed idea of human nature. I wasn't the person I had been when I was working at the bank. My priorities were different. There was hope in that. There is no hope in a fixed idea of human nature. Besides whose human nature are we talking about? Pat Tillman's? Ronald Reagan's? The people who let me stay in their homes within twenty-four hours of meeting me?

Perryville was an *Orange Is the New Black*–style prison. There are no cells, other than solitary confinement, and the women have "privileges" higher-security prisoners don't. Cots outfitted with individual TV sets fill a large common area with concrete floors and easy-access showers and libraries. There was no privacy, though, much like the military when you're deployed. The women worked for the highway department during the day and socialized freely at night within the prison. I spent almost an hour with them after my talk.

A tall woman named Marissa with a reddish-brown buzz cut came up to me and said, "I thought your talk was interesting and Pat Tillman was great, but I feel like you could go farther in what you're saying. You can have all the positive thoughts in the world, but if you're poor and there is no opportunity to not be poor, you get desperate. You do desperate things. This is something that people with money don't understand, or don't want to understand. And I think that is why most of us are in here. . . . When there are no jobs or financial hope for people, they do whatever they have to do to survive. And if you notice, most of the women here aren't white and none of them are rich."

"I know I should be talking more about that type of thing, but it's hard."

"I understand. . . . Just try and talk more about people in prison when you talk—because ain't none of us got a voice in here, and that's the way they like it."

GILA BEND, AZ | Mile 2,707

Population 1,872 | Est. 1980

I walked with the salamanders the next day. They were as numerous as mice in the rice fields of Arkansas, but much more fun to watch. They zipped back and forth on two of their four legs without much deliberation.

Shed snakeskins and the soft crumbling of abandoned creature dens detailed my path through the desert. I was paralleling Interstate 8 a half-mile from the road. I didn't think I was legally allowed to walk on the interstate, based on past experience, so I was essentially hiding. The ground was flat and hard except for the snake and jackrabbit holes—which were numerous.

I was less than 270 miles to the Pacific.

I saw my first rattlesnake and my first Border Patrol agents the next day. Both were surprisingly receptive. The rattler was sunning itself and barely flinched when I walked within a few feet. The Border Patrol agents hopped the center median in two white-and-green trucks with jail cells mounted on the beds, their red and blue lights pulsing, and nearly drove through a barbed-wire fence when they saw me collecting firewood a few hundred yards from the road. Smiling, I walked up to them, using my staff as a surrender symbol, and said, "I guess my silhouette fits a certain profile out here, doesn't it?" They were quickly disarmed by my complexion.

I cleaned up camp the next morning, clipped the belt buckle on my pack, and started toward the road. I soon noticed four eyes crouched behind a bush. I moved closer and, like jackrabbits, two teenage boys in jeans and black T-shirts ran north over a nearby sand dune. I pictured the boys sitting anxiously behind the next bush feeling, certain our encounter meant their demise. It seemed the two had run across a moderately secure international border under a desert full moon, without backpacks. I was impressed. I nearly doubled back to share water and exchange notes, but saw a Border Patrol agent less than a mile away. I waved and said only, "Good morning!" Walkers don't expose other walkers' hiding spots.

10

California

FELICITY, CA | Mile 2,851

Population 2 | Est. 1986

The official center of the world, or universe, if you'd like, is a dot on a bronze plaque within a polished granite pyramid in Felicity, California. You'd think the center of the world would be buzzing with activity; it wasn't. The site was empty: no humans, no animals, no trees. Only granite landmarks scattered throughout a large three- or four-acre plot. There was the pyramid that housed the plaque. There was a green sign that said "Population 2." The gnomon of a fifteen-foot sundial, a bronze of Michelangelo's *Arm of God*, pointed to the Church on the Hill, the highest point in town. There was a sculpture at the entrance of the church, made from a twenty-five-foot-high section of the original stairway of the Eiffel Tower, removed by the French government in 1983. An abbreviated history of humanity was etched in twenty-yard slabs of polished granite. All this against a backdrop of dust, sand, and tumbleweed. Felicity's mission is that it "forever remain a town of uninhibited imagination." This two-person town was built to last, and it probably will. One could imagine that generations from now people will look at these "monuments" and try to glean something about what life was like in the United States at the turn of the twenty-first century. I think they will learn a lot—and I doubt they will be impressed. Polished granite pyramids, bronze arms of God, and a church for passing tourists, regardless of the size and beauty, can feel like litter without a society or culture to support them.

Former Chicago Bear Bob Kilcullen, who I met at the NFL Alumni Association, called a friend at the *Chicago Sun-Times* about doing a story on the walk. Rick Telander arrived at the center of the world with his Eddie Bauer backpack, notepad, and worn-out knees to walk with me in the desert for a few days. We talked all day. It was a welcome distraction from the 102-degree heat. Rick was a cornerback for Northwestern and has written eight books, including the acclaimed *Heaven Is a Playground.* If the walls of the old Chicago Stadium, Yankee Stadium, and the Boston Garden could speak, they would be less interesting than Rick. But he mostly asked me questions. We stopped at the trailer outposts for the All-American Canal project and the Canadian Gas Company. We met dozens of employees and savored the air conditioning and cold water at each stop.

We walked on a pressed sand road a few yards south of Interstate 8 and a hundred yards from the fifteen-foot-tall fence that divides Mexico and the United States. Between the sand road and I-8 lie industrial-strength white bike racks, Lego-shaped concrete blocks, and ocean-liner chains. The second wall, I would later be told, was to keep drug runners and coyotes who drove through the first wall from entering I-8.

THE DUNES, CA | Mile 2,871

Jerry Vines, a seventy-eight-year-old Korean War veteran and park host at Buttercup RV park, helped fellow RVers and dune-buggy enthusiasts when they ran into trouble. As an unofficial undercover Border Patrol agent, he also watched over the dunes at night. Thanks to Jerry's vigilance, many unsuspecting drug runners and immigrants have been rounded up—he was proud of himself.

"I sit and watch for 'em day and night. We don't have enough people manning this border like we should, so I do my duty and volunteer. I can enjoy the outdoors, live out my retirement, and serve my country," said Jerry.

I looked out and saw nothing but sand. Jerry thought he was keeping us safe. He was old, and I was happy to enjoy his shade and lawn chair. Rick and I listened to Jerry talk for a few hours. I never asked Jerry about NAFTA, the wars that were fought to stretch the US border over his lawn chairs and RV, or why people needed to leave their families and run through a desert or swim across a dangerous man-made canal—one the All-American Canal company refuses to outfit with ladders to save the lives of the many border crossers who drown there each year—to work the worst jobs. You pick and choose your debates a bit more carefully in the dessert—the home of all things banished.

Rick and I found a place to camp not too far from Jerry, two hundred yards off the interstate. We were guarded by the huge dunes used to film the opening scene from *Return of the Jedi*. We built a bonfire. We talked politics, religion, and books well into the night.

EL CENTRO, CA | Mile 2,959

Population 42,598 | Est. 1906

The sun was buried deep in the horizon and a faint orange glow was all that remained of the day. I was slicing through fragrant alfalfa fields on abandoned railroad tracks when Philippe and Rachel pulled up alongside me in a white pickup. They were both immigrants. I lifted my head from the email I was reading on my BlackBerry to hear Philippe say, "We saw you in the paper and wanted to bring you water."

I left the tracks and walked down a small hill to meet them. I thanked them, said goodbye, and ran up to the point where I left the tracks. Calmly coiled in the center of the tracks like three feet of uncooked Italian sausage was a rattlesnake. Reading the email in the near-darkness, I would have stepped on the snake and been bitten if it were not for Rachel and Philippe.

Farm Workers: Sí Se Puede

"*Sí se puede, sí, sí se puede!*" was the slogan of the National Farm Workers Association (NFWA). César Chávez, along with Dolores Huerta, formed the organization in California in 1962.

"I see us as one family. We cannot turn our backs on each other and our future. We farm workers are closest to food production. We were the first to recognize the serious health hazards of agriculture pesticides to both consumers and ourselves," Chávez said in his famous "Wrath of Grapes" speech in 1986.

Chávez, Huerta, and the leaders of the NFWA and United Farm Workers (UFW) knew growers had a history of dividing workers by race in order to break field strikes, so they emphasized the inherent strength of large, unified numbers across racial lines when trying to win demands. They had done this before, in 1970.

The NFWA sought to ban poisonous pesticides that were making three hundred thousand of the four million farm workers in the US sick. Filipinos and Mexicans alike were losing hands, passing along birth defects to their children, and dying young from cancer. The fruit and vegetable growers were also passing along these poisonous chemicals to their consumers.[25]

During the strike, growers hired *braceros* (Spanish for "arms"), workers brought up from Mexico by the US government. They worked for much less pay than US-born workers. Growers kept braceros under the constant threat of deportation if they complained, and they were at regular odds with the strikers. Chávez and Huerta responded by organizing a three-hundred-mile walk with thousands of farm workers from Delano, California, to Sacramento, California. The voting-rights marches from Selma to Montgomery inspired the walk. Chávez drew further attention to the strike and discouraged outbursts of violence by striking farm workers by enduring a twenty-five-day fast, during which he lost thirty-five pounds.

These actions inspired 12 percent of the people in the United States, a total of seventeen million people, to boycott California grapes until the demands of the UFW were met. Other unions, church activists, students, and civil rights groups all enthusiastically backed the boycott. This boycott helped connect working-class families in urban areas with rural farm worker families. After a five-year strike and boycott, they won their first union contracts, which earned them better pay, benefits, protections, and ended the use of chemicals like DDT. It became the most famous workers' boycott in US history.[26]

The growers were back with new poisons in the eighties. Again Chávez and Huerta, using the same tactics, appealed to consumers to support the union by boycotting grapes, lettuce, and wine. New insecticides similar to nerve gas were poisoning workers. Workers were again contracting cancer, losing limbs, and having children with birth defects. These tactics proved successful for a second time. They won contracts that banned the five most poisonous insecticides.

The union was always a step ahead of the federal government in demanding that poisons be banned. These boycotts led to the Agricultural Labor Relations Act, which granted farm workers the right to organize and bargain for better wages and working conditions, as well as a ban on the most dangerous insecticides of the day.[27]

The UFW became a model for how to build a union among the most exploited workers. If farm workers could organize and win, so can retail workers and minimum-wage fast-food workers, which would help lessen the giant wealth and power divide in this country.

SALVATION MOUNTAIN, CA | Mile 2,959

Population 1 | Est. 1996

> *Our original guiding stars are struggle and hope. But there is no such thing as a lone struggle, no such thing as a lone hope.*
>
> **—Pablo Neruda**

Haydee Rodriguez, a high-school literature teacher, invited me to talk at her school—which turned out to be a full assembly of more than three hundred students. Afterward, Haydee and I went out to dinner. I ordered a beer. She said she didn't drink anymore.

"My dad left my mom a few months before I was born," Haydee said. "I felt incomplete because of it, but learning to recognize that incompleteness is what taught me to feel whole. I don't know if that makes sense."

"So there is the ideal Haydee and then there is the Haydee I am talking to?"

"Mourning the death of my ideal self, or a woman that grew up with a father, helps me. My past will always be attached to me. Accepting that reality, as opposed to what I would ideally like myself to be, is what has allowed me to see the world and become a good teacher," she said. "The thing is, Rory, we are all incomplete. I am, you are, this country certainly is. We need to accept that about ourselves. By appreciating our own incompleteness, we can see and respect what is incomplete about others—and then we don't try to fill ourselves in with the wrong thing."

We finished dinner, and Haydee said she wanted to take me to Salvation Mountain the next day. I asked what Salvation Mountain was. She said it was a surprise, but something I should see.

"God speaks to me through my rib. He told me where to find the material to make Salvation Mountain. I have been here for thirty years and it's starting to receive a lot of attention. It's in the Internet," Leonard Knight said a day later. It is. Sean Penn found Salvation Mountain on the Internet and used it for a scene in *Into the Wild.*

Seventy-seven-year-old Leonard had been building a four-story adobe-and-hay-bale monument to his mantra, "God Is Love," for more than thirty years. Using the color scheme of a gumball machine and the blueprints for a mound of mashed potatoes, Leonard inspired dozens of visitors a day. Passages from the King James Bible, along with his favorite "untoiling or spinning symbol," a flower, ornamented the mountain. The flowers were made with globs of adobe and Leonard's pressing fist. With a New England accent he said, "I can make three hundred flowers a day." Leonard woke up at four each morning and lugged gallons of paint and buckets of adobe up ladders and through a maze of caves. Battling the desert sun, he tirelessly repainted. Leonard slept in his truck when it was cold and on a tattered couch beside it when it was warm. He wore a light blue mechanic's jumpsuit and a Quaker-brimmed straw hat; both were flecked with the colors of the mountain.

I looked up and saw the giant words "God Is Love" painted in red in a rolled-dough font on the cap of the mountain. Leonard had struggled to keep his land. According to Leonard's assistant Chey, the town of Slab City has cited him for environmental violations associated with the lead paint he used a few decades back and tried to have the hill demolished. Pro-love lawyers intervened and were able to legally designate the mountain a national folk-art landmark. Leonard's dream will probably never be touched by the town or state.

After our tour Haydee and I headed back to the car.

"What Leonard is doing out here is strange and exhilarating to see, but it's kind of sad, isn't it?" Haydee said.

"Part of me is jealous. I wouldn't mind staying out here with Leonard. To be honest, I wouldn't mind dying here," I replied.

"To be content building a giant boob in the dessert has its

lure, doesn't it? I'm not saying this isn't what Leonard needs to do or should be doing, or that people aren't inspired by it, but it seems to me that all this work is pretty self-indulgent."

"You are the smartest, best, and kindest person in the room when you are the only one in the room . . . or the desert."

"Yeah. I think so, but some people need it that way," she said. "It's important that we figure out our limitations and then embrace them. It's clear that Leonard has a degree of self-possession that is enviable. He knows what he wants to do and he is committed to that—but let's not call him a saint or anything like that. Leonard is clearly working out some issues. And he will probably die trying to work out his issues. And I think that is the most courageous thing in the world. But wouldn't it be great to truly see your issues in the context of other people's issues? I think there is more to it than spending all your time in the dessert—at least for people besides Leonard."

Haydee dropped me off where she picked me up and I headed out toward the ocean for my last few days of walking. The final night of the walk. I camped on top of a lush green hill outside of San Diego. It was a quiet night. I looked at the prayer card I had carried since the second day—Jonathan's prayer card, given to me by his sister. He had been dead nine months when I received the card. On that hill he had been dead almost eighteen months. I buried it on top of the hill. I don't know why I did that. I don't know why I did a lot of things.

I decided I couldn't officially complete the walk that night. I didn't know how I could keep walking, but I knew I had to—and the best way to do that would be not to finish.

OCEANSIDE, CA | Mile 3,087

Population 183,095 | Est. 1888

I passed Sea World and its killer whales. The air became heavier and ocean mist swirled in front of me. I expelled a final heavy breath at the top of my last small hill. The patchwork of colors I remembered from the pull-down world map in my fifth-grade social-studies class appeared before my eyes. I thought of the 195 other countries I hadn't walked across.

A few dozen people met me at the beach: people who had followed the walk through my blog, people I had never met. They were strangers who didn't feel like strangers. They held signs and cheered like we had known each other a long time.

People from San Diego and Oceanside were there; so were a few news cameras. A family I'd met in Arizona drove five hours to meet me. My dad was there and so was his friend Jim. Kate was waiting for me back home. She couldn't take time off work and we couldn't afford a plane ticket at that point, but I was thinking about her. I asked someone to count out forty-two steps from the water line.

The sun glowed through a light haze and the lip of the Pacific Ocean said, "What are you waiting for?" I was now forty-two yards from what I had spent the last eight months dreaming of—a finish line. Forty-two was the number on the white hat the Foundation sent me before the walk. I'd worn it every day. Now it was a desert color, coated in soot, sweat, and oil. Forty-two was the number on Pat Tillman's Arizona State jersey. Some would say the $3.6 million Pat turned down was a finish line. My line seemed microscopic compared to the one he stopped just short of.

The crowd started chanting, "Jump! Jump! Jump!" They wanted me to jump into the water—but I couldn't. To me, the water represented the end.

I didn't need an end. I needed a beginning.

I was scared I was going to sink back into a dead-eyed routine, like I had at the bank before the walk. I was scared that I would get home and sit in a chair in front of some TV, thinking about all the great people I met the one time I had done something. And it would be over. I was different, but for the most part the world was the same as it was before the walk—the economic imbalance, the lack of democracy, the systematic oppression, they were all still there. I wasn't ready for the closure that finishing the walk might give me. The only thing I knew for sure, staring at that water, was that the world was worth fighting for. I was now confident that most of the people in the world were good, and that those people did their best to make the world a better place with the knowledge they had, in the little free time they could afford. I also knew that I didn't know how to make things any better for a world that was still awfully imbalanced.

The end of the walk was the end of my belief that I could change the world on my own. Crossing the finish line by myself seemed to betray this newfound realization. Stopping short was symbolic. Maybe it was only a symbol to me. I knew that this journey wasn't something one person could ever finish alone. But I needed to the strength to say that out loud.

I raised forty-five thousand dollars for the Pat Tillman Foundation—not much for eight months of walking. I had different thoughts about charity by then, too. The Latin American writer and activist Eduardo Galeano once called charity "too vertical." He meant that charity flows from the top to the bottom—but the solidarity I experienced on the walk was a joining together of equals.

I didn't touch the ocean. I gave a small speech—and stopped. And the road opened wide.

Acknowledgements

There are so many people to thank. I need at least a thousand pages to acknowledge all the wonderful people who supported me, as well as the Pat Tillman Foundation.

Let me start with the people who helped get this book published. Thank you to Jon Kurinsky for your insightful, multilayered, and pro bono edit. It was invaluable. Thank you to Sarah Grey for your encouragement and amazing edit. I am so lucky this book found its way to you! Every writer deserves an editor as smart and author-friendly as you. Thank you to Sarah Macaraeg for helping me to get the ball rolling. Your edits helped me get this unwieldy project to a manageable state. Thank you to Julie Fain for believing in the book and making it a reality. I will be forever grateful. Thank you to Anthony Arnove for getting behind the book and for all your work in making Haymarket such a respected publisher. Thank you to Ahmed Shawki for making Haymarket the publisher it is today. Thank you to Jim Plank and Jason Farbman for your work in getting the book noticed and your enthusiastic support. Thank you to Rachel Cohen for your positive encouragement and tireless efforts making sure the book was put together properly. Thank you to Brenda Coughlin for your encouragement, your support, and the amazing work you do. Thank you to all the wonderful people at the Lannan Foundation. Thank you to Eric Ruder for the terrific cover design. And thank you to the rest of my friends at Haymarket: John McDonald, Eric Kerl, Daphne Jackson, and Jesus Ramos.

Thank you to Rick Telander. You are a constant source of inspiration and a true friend. Thank you to Neil Steinberg for your kind words and encouragement. Thank you to Lee Sustar for motivating me to finish this book. Thank you to Dave Zirin. You are a huge force for good in the world and your writing is a regular motivation. Thank you to Keeanga-Yamahtta Taylor for your commitment to making the world a better place and for putting in a good word for me at Haymarket. I've learned so much from you. Thank you to Joe Allen for all your support. Thank you to Will Hettinger for your useful thoughts on the book. Thank you to Dan Sharber for your excellent read-through. Thank you to Heather and Brent Lindon for your help in so many ways. Thank you to Ryan Fanning. I couldn't ask for a better brother. Thank you to my dad, Bob Fanning, for instilling a sense of adventure in me. Thank you to my mom, Lynn Poepp, for all your energy, love, empathy, and patience. Thank you to Ken Poepp for your generosity and kind spirit. Thank you to Diane, Don, Kyle, and Kellen Kmiecik. Thank you to Wendy, Wayne, Vern, and Sue Burton. Thank you to Great-Aunt Pat. Thank you to Jan and Lee Kooi. Thank you to Mary, Gregg, and Cord Kirchhoefer. You helped shape the walk in such a positive way. Thank you to Laura, Quinn, Patrick, and Daniel Fanning. Thank you to Joyce, Andrew, and Tim Fanning. Thank you to Chris van Benthuysen, Stacy Kuta van Benthuysen, and Matt Pritzel. Thank you to Tasos Foukas.

Thank you to Usber Lopez. Thank you to Laurie, Soleil, and Destiny. Thank you, Colleen Collins. Thank you, Luther, Stewart, and Sara from Walhalla, South Carolina. Thank you to Vickie Atwood-Romine from Florence, Alabama. Thank you to Tomeka from Biscoe, Arkansas. Thank you to Lindsey Kirk Martindale. Thank you to Hampton Inn. Thank you to the Riley family from North Little Rock, Arkansas. You are such a beautiful and loving family. Thank you to Mrs. Valentine. Thank you to all the wonderful members of the Everhart family. Thank you to Ryan Orrell, who organized so much for me in Hot Springs, Arkansas. You deserve your own chapter. Thank you to Bridget and Marty from Caddo Gap, Arkansas. You deserve your own chapter, too. You are such amazing people. Thank you for putting me up for more than a week and for all the driving! Thank you to Billy's Guitar Shop in Glenwood, Arkansas. Thank you to Jim McCarthy for your generosity. Thank you to Cindy and Sandy outside of Glenwood, Arkansas. Thank you Bill Barnes, Jim Mishler, Carla Gadbury, and Kathy Holt. Thank you to the Wilcox family in Cerro Gordo, Oklahoma. Thank you to Chris Willingham. Thank you to Jimmy Tapley and Rachel. Thank you Bryan Scott, and the Flippen family from Fort Worth, Texas. Thank you Bill and Laverne from Paris, Texas. Thank you to Jerry and Daniel Kramer. Thank you Kenny Smith and Annie Golightly. You will always be larger than life, Annie. Thank you Jerald and Elaine Thomas from Commerce, Texas. Thank you to Jen Walter: you will always be an inspiration. Thank you Rory and Amanda McCarthy. I had a blast with you guys! Thank you to Dave Savino. Thank you Nina and Michael. I hope you are doing well. Thank you to Jane, Ruby, and Jimmy Baldwin. Thank you to Alison, David, Jett, Chloe, and Miles Adams. Thank you to Shai Berry. Thank you to Lauri from Anson. Thank you to Michelle Terry and Roby High School. Thank you to Jacob Crawford and Joshua from Snyder, Texas. Thank you Marianne Randals. Thank you to Bob Kilcullen and Bill Gleason. You will always be remembered. Thank you to Dwayne West and Pete Harland from Lubbock. Thank you to John Dewitt. Thank you to Michael, Logan, and Stephen from Texas Tech. Thank you to Rachel Sherrod. Thank you to Children's Hope. Thank you to Ed Gleason. Thank you to Sonia Garcia. Thank you to Chris Seuffert for helping to kick-off this thing. Thank you to Norah Parker. Thank you to Dr. Andrew Weil. Thank you to Elija Mendez and his parents. Thank you to Joseph Campbell. Thank you to Joe, Stella, and Mark from Tangle Y in Hondo, New Mexico. Thank you to Kathy from Pie Town, New Mexico. Thank you Karen, Tina, Connie, and Dave from Show Low, Arizona. Thank you to the Black Mesa Hot Shots. Thank you Traci, Terri, Don, and Dean from Payson Rim Country in Arizona. Thank you Bruce and Paige Snyder. Thank you to Carolyn Pendergast. I'll never forget all the help you gave me! Thank you to the outstanding LeBlanc family: Mauri, Cindy, Jake, and Brady. You guys are awesome. Thank you to Charlie Huebner and Marlon Shirley. Thank you to Jennifer Kushman. You are so generous. Thank you to Libby Anderson. Thank you to Jody, Tia, Pat, and Sally from Yuma. Thank you to Haydee Rodriguez. I miss you all and look forward to seeing everyone again in the near future.

Thank you to Anand Gopal for writing the best book I have read on Afghanistan: *No Good Men Among the Living: America, the Taliban, and the War through Afghan Eyes.*

Thank you to Kate Fanning. You are all of my strength. I am

so grateful you are in my life. Thank you to Greta Fanning. You are my entire world.

Thank you to everyone at the Pat Tillman Foundation, past and present. Thank you especially to Marie Tillman.

And thank you to Kevin and Mary Tillman. You continue to be a tremendous inspiration.

Notes

1. Nat Turner, *The Confessions of Nat Turner and Related Documents*, ed. Kenneth S. Greenberg (New York: Bedford/St. Martin's, 1996).
2. Patricia C. McKissack and Fredrick L. McKissack, *Rebels Against Slavery: American Slave Revolts* (New York: Scholastic, 1999).
3. Quoted in Richard Seymour, *American Insurgents: A Brief History of American Empire* (Chicago: Haymarket Books, 2012), 18.
4. Jen Marlowe, Martina Davis-Correia, and Troy Anthony Davis, *I Am Troy Davis* (Chicago: Haymarket Books, 2013).
5. Stanley Howard, "They Killed Him with the Whole World Watching," *Socialist Worker,* October 17, 2013, http://socialistworker.org/2013/10/17/they-killed-him-as-the-world-watched.
6. Marlene Martin, "We Are Still Troy Davis," *Socialist Worker,* September 21, 2012, http://socialistworker.org/2012/09/20/we-are-still-troy-davis.
7. David Grossman, *On Killing* (Boston: Back Bay Books, 2009), 25.
8. Ibid., 21.
9. Christina Bergmark, "The Scottsboro Boys Case," *Socialist Worker,* December 1985.
10. "Ida B Wells and the Long Fight Against Lynching in the US South," *Socialist Worker UK,* http://socialistworker.co.uk/art/34642/Ida+B+Wells+and+the+long+fight+against+lynching+in+the+US+South.
11. Ida B. Wells-Barnett, *The Red Record: Tabulated Statistics and Alleged Causes of Lynching in the United States,* 1895, http://www.gutenberg.org/files/14977/14977-h/14977-h.htm.
12. Ibid., preface.
13. Ibid.
14. Jason M. Breslow, "By the Numbers: Childhood Poverty in the U.S.,"

PBS, November 20, 2012, http://www.pbs.org/wgbh/pages/frontline/social-issues/poor-kids/by-the-numbers-childhood-poverty-in-the-u-s.

15. Helen Scott, "The Mark Twain They Didn't Teach Us in School," *International Socialist Review* 10 (Winter 2000): 61–65.
16. US Army, "Ranger Creed," http://www.goarmy.com/ranger/heritage/ranger-creed.html.
17. Ward Churchill, *A Little Matter of Genocide* (San Francisco: City Lights Books, 1998).
18. Paul Voss's grandfather's best friend was Manfred von Richthofen, otherwise known as the Red Baron. They were both German fighter pilots during World War I. The Red Baron is credited with eighty air-combat victories, the most of any fighter pilot during that war.
19. Seven times the number of troops died from disease than from battle during the Mexican-American War.
20. Sandy Boyer, "Defying a War of Conquest," *Socialist Worker,* March 19, 2010, http://socialistworker.org/2010/03/19/defying-a-war-of-conquest.
21. Ibid.
22. Gregg Doyel, "NFL Is Killing Its Players, and League Doesn't Care," CBS Sports, December 23, 2010, www.cbssports.com/nfl/story/14477196/nfl-is-killing-its-players-and-league-doesnt-care.
23. PBS Newshour, "House Investigates Army's Handling of Tillman, Lynch Incidents," transcript, April 24, 2007, http://www.pbs.org/newshour/bb/military/jan-june07/tillman_04-24.html.
24. *Indian Country Today* Staff, "Fight the Power: 100 Heroes of Native Resistance, Part I," *Indian Country Today*, July 24, 2013, http://indiancountrytodaymedianetwork.com/2013/07/24/fight-power-100-heroes-native-resistance-part-1-150552.
25. United Farm Workers, "History," 2006, http://www.ufw.org/_page.php?inc=history/07.html&menu=research.
26. Frank Bardacke, *Trampling Out the Vintage: Cesar Chavez and the Two Souls of the United Farm Workers* (New York: Verso, 2011).
27. Michele Bollinger and Dao X. Tran, eds., *101 Changemakers: Rebels and Radicals Who Changed US History* (Chicago: Haymarket Books, 2012).

Index

"Passim" (literally "scattered") indicates intermittent discussion of a topic over a cluster of pages.

© Bridget Nameche

About the Author

Rory Fanning walked across the United States for the Pat Tillman Foundation in 2008 and 2009, following two deployments to Afghanistan with the Second Army Ranger Battalion. He is a housing activist living in Chicago, Illinois, and works for Haymarket Books. This is his first book.